All is Grace

C000145079

Henri Boulad is rapidly becoming ̲
spiritual figures of our age. Born in
Jesuit and studied in France, Lebanon and the United States. He
worked in the slums, and among lepers and the sick, and has also
been involved in pioneering education projects, but he is best
known for his lectures. Some are given on his travels, but he also
delivers a regular series of open lectures in Alexandria. It is out of
one such series that this book has arisen.

All is Grace deals with one of the most basic of all questions:
the nature of time. In a series of brilliant meditations, Fr Boulad
discusses scientific problems of time and relativity, the nature of
the present, eternity, coping with the past, redeeming time and facing
the future – all with an attractive informality which sometimes
disguises just how deep are the problems with which he is
concerned.

No narrow pietist, but well aware of the world around him, Fr
Boulad shows the range of his sympathies by the scope of his
quotations – Sartre, Nietzsche, Katzantzakis, Saint-Exupéry and
Bonhoeffer. There is something in his writings for everyone not
only to meditate on but to live by.

HENRI BOULAD

All is Grace
God and the Mystery of Time

SCM PRESS

Translated by John Bowden from the German
Alles ist Gnade, Der Mensch und das Mysterium der Zeit,
edited and translated by Hidda Westenberger,
published by Herold Druck- und Verlagsgesellschaft, Vienna,
and the French *L'homme et le mystère du temps*,
published by Téqui, Paris.

© Herold Druck- und Verlagsgesellschaft 1988

Translation © Crossroad Publishing Company 1991

All rights reserved. No part of this publication may be
reproduced, stored in a retrieval system, or transmitted,
in any form or by any means, electronic, mechanical,
photocopying, recording or otherwise, without the prior
written permission of the publisher, SCM Press Ltd.

British Library Cataloguing in Publication Data
Boulad, Henri
  All is grace: God and the mystery of time.
  1. Time. Philosophical perspectives
  I. Title II. Alles ist Gnade, der Mensch und das Mysterium
  der Zeit. *English*
  115
  ISBN 0–334–01876–5

First published in English 1991
by SCM Press Ltd
26–30 Tottenham Road, London N1 4BZ

Phototypeset by Input Typesetting Ltd, London
and printed in Great Britain by
Billing and Sons Ltd Worcester

Contents

1 There are Many Different Times

'They say that I am thirty years old. But if I had lived three minutes in one minute, would I not be ninety years old now?' (*Charles Baudelaire*)

If I asked you whether you knew what time was, you would reply, 'Yes, certainly!' 'All right,' I might say, 'then what *is* time?' At that point you would probably begin to hesitate and would have to think very hard before making a reply. We think we know what time is, and hold on to this belief until we are asked to put it clearly into words. And that's where the trouble starts.

Time is a bit like existence or space. It is one of those realities that is so natural, so everyday, so ordinary, in which we are so steeped that we do not know exactly what they are. If I asked you 'What is space?' you would find it difficult to tell me. If I asked you 'What is existence?' you would not know what to say. I live, I exist, I am, but what does that mean? What is the space within which I move? What is the time within which I develop?

If you could ask a fish 'What is water?', it would tell you, 'I don't know, I've never seen it, I don't know what you're talking about.' Why? Because it's there; it's what the fish lives in.

To know what time is we need to be outside time. To know what water is, we have to be outside water. We need a certain detachment, a certain distance, if we are to know and understand anything. Where there is total coincidence and total immersion, knowledge is impossible. There must be a distance.

I only began to discover and slowly to get to know Egypt the day I left it. That's when I began to say, 'So that's what Egypt is...' It had become too much part of me for me to be able to know it while I continued to live there. I could never have pictured it unless I had spent many years far from it. While one is within something, one does not know what it means. We only come to know about childhood when we stop being children.

When I talk about love and sexuality, people say to me, 'What do you know about that? How can you talk about something which you've excluded from your life by becoming a priest?' My reply is: 'That's true, but precisely because I am detached from this reality, I may perhaps be able to talk about it better, since I can see it more clearly from a distance and notice some aspects of it better than if I were immersed in it.'

Now if all that I have just said is true, the question arises: 'How can we talk about time if we are completely immersed in it?' But are we so sure that we are completely immersed in time? Animals, plants and even more minerals are certainly immersed totally in time, but part of our being is outside time, above it – otherwise, we could not know what time is, nor could we talk about it.

Human beings are both immersed in time and yet emerge above it. This detachment from time and from ourselves, this capacity to move in and out of time, we call consciousness.

If we are conscious beings, it is because we can see ourselves and think about ourselves. We have an inner space which is the result of a 'step towards reflection', an evolutionary stage that we went through three or four million years ago. Within us we have space to think and reflect. The word 'reflection' is itself significant. It suggests a mirror deep within us in which we look at ourselves, in which we 'reflect' ourselves. If I were stuck to the mirror there would be no reflection; there is a reflection only because there is some distance. The distance is the necessary condition for the images that we make of ourselves, for the awareness of ourselves that we acquire.

Here are some words of Henri Simon, a contemporary French philosopher:

Human beings are animals who can remember and foresee. Because they remember, it is natural for them to reflect and regret. Because they foresee, it is natural for them to fear and hope.

Moreover, it is because human beings have a memory that they can engage in forward planning. It is because they can recall the past to their consciousness that they can project themselves into the future and have a notion of time.

If they lived consciously only in the present, then they would be no more than an absurd series of discontinuous eternities in which they would have neither a sense of personal unity nor the conditions for coherent, active and creative thought.

Let me make some brief comments.

Human memory is the sign of this distance which is to be found within us. When I talk about things in the past, I establish a distance from the present in which I live. So I am not stuck to the present. Moreover, words are the expression of this distance: to express ourselves is to detach ourselves from what we are and to project ourselves forward.

Human beings, I said, are beings who remember. One of our deepest and sweetest joys is to recall old memories. 'Do you remember when...? Those were the days...' And because we remember, we are also beings who reflect and who regret – hence the sense of nostalgia. Animals do not regret, do not have any sense of nostalgia, because they do not have this distance within them.

Finally, human beings foresee: they have a sense of the future, and animals do not. Even the ant in La Fontaine's fable which stores up provisions for the winter does not do so out of foresight, but quite automatically, and by instinct. Because human beings are capable of foresight, it is normal for them to fear and hope.

Human beings are the only animals capable of conscious anxiety and deep care. Why? Because they are torn between their past, which is no longer, and their future, which has yet to come and which they hope for. This tension within them creates an uncertainty and an anxiety which are utterly unknown in the animal world. More than at any other stage in the past, human beings now have an acute sense of their history. The past has never been as present as it is now; history has never been so studied as it is in our day. On the other hand, people have never talked so much as they do today about the future, have never been so concerned to discover what it will bring. And that is the reason why men and women are anxious beings, full of deep disquiet.

Time is not just a series of particular moments, but it is a duration which I assume, because I take a detached position over against my own life.

Human beings are the only animals who know that they are born and who know that they will die, who know that they have begun and who know that they will come to an end, that this is only a 'matter of time'. Beyond question that is the ultimate source of their disquiet and their anxiety.

All animals are born and all animals die. But human beings know only that they have been born. Of course they do not remember being born. I do not suppose that you have any recollection of your birth, though psychoanalysts tell us that the trauma of birth is engraved on our subconsciousness. However, this is not a memory. So I know that I began, that I was born, and I also know that I will come to an end, that I will die. There is no doubt that this death is the greatest question-mark over our lives, the deepest source of our anguish.

The emergence of human beings above their history and their life is the sign of a transcendence over all other realities in the world. This transcendence seems to me to be convincing proof that because we are above time, we are also beyond time, and that means that we do not die completely. Something in us escapes time: part of us, the essential part of us, our self, that which makes me 'me', escapes the flux of time.

As a human being, I am like a traveller standing on a station platform and watching a train go past. The train arrives and departs, but I remain on the station. I look at my life and my history in just the same way. From the fact that I can contemplate my life, I can affirm that in some way I am beyond my life, and therefore beyond my death.

The fact that I am aware of my death is the sign of my transcendence over this event which affects only part of me, the more external part. The essential part of me, what I really am, is unaffected and remains above all this; and that is the case even now. Fr Maurice Zundel comments:

> There is within us an inner permanence by which, in a timeless present, we gather together the fleeting moments whose fate would otherwise be to be lost irrevocably in the stream of time. The stream of time would wash everything away, were there not something above it which prevented all phenomena from slowly sinking into it and dissolving. We would not know that we have to pass away one day if we passed on completely, just as we do not notice the movement of the earth which carries us round with its own motion.

Indeed we cannot sense the rotation of the earth. But why? Because we are caught up in it ourselves. To sense that the earth is rotating, we have to be above it. Similarly, since we feel that our life is running out and that time is passing, we are above that flux which carries us on towards death. We are beyond our deaths and transcend our destinies.

So there is a kind of opposition between time which runs out and escapes us – which brings with it ageing, decrepitude and death – and our inner time, which is spiritual time. This is the time of our consciousness, which develops slowly and, from all that fails and passes away, builds itself up towards a culmination and a fullness of its own. So that means that there are two times: a time which passes away, and the time that will always remain with me, the time which I myself am.

So if in some respects death is catastrophe and annihilation, in other respects it is a consummation and fulfilment of human beings, their realization. As Fr Zundel comments:

> Physical death thus coincides with the explosion of an inner life which has achieved its full maturity and is totally freed from time, so that it now surpasses its own limits.

He goes on to make a comparison between a lecture or a speech, which passes away, and its meaning, which remains. If I talk to you for quarter of an hour, you have heard a certain number of words; however, within these words you may have caught something meaningful which will always stay with you. What I said may already belong to the past, but its meaning can remain present and escape temporality. So human beings can be like the meaning of these words which are comparable to their own lives and their own history: their lives, their history, pass away, but they themselves remain.

If we go to a concert we pay attention, listen, enjoy, from the first note to the last. At the end we say, 'What a pity it's over'. But in fact nothing is over, since the whole marvellous concert is contained within us, deep down, in a sphere outside time. Zundel ends by saying:

> There would be neither speech nor music if the dead syllables and the dead notes did not survive in a consciousness which does not pass away at all. Time makes sense only outside time.

By dominating time, though a whole part of our being is nevertheless immersed within it, we human beings demonstrate our fundamental transcendence over the course of time and over our whole environment. We are not imprisoned in time, just as we are not imprisoned in space. The best part of us, the essential part of us, emerges above the flux which carries us away, or which seems to carry us away.

Memory bears witness that we shall not die completely with the fleeting moment. This survival, precarious and limited though it may seem at first sight, would be inconceivable if it did not become part of our 'abiding memories'.

Let us now reflect more deeply on these two notions of time: superficial, external, objective time and internal, personal, subjective time.

Objective time is of linear duration and can be measured by the clock or the calendar. It is five o'clock, six o'clock, seven o'clock, eight o'clock. Each successive hour is of just the same kind as the previous hour and all previous hours; it, too, consists of sixty minutes, and each of these minutes consists of sixty seconds. The same goes for the calendar. Monday, Tuesday, Thursday, any day, each has the same duration, exactly twenty-four hours. Months follow months and years follow years. We spontaneously think of this kind of time when anyone talks of time: it is always the 'external' time of the clock and the calendar, a sequence of measurable moments, from a temporal perspective each precisely the same.

However, modern scientists assure us that this time, which seems to us to be perfectly objective, clear and measurable, is in fact a very relative concept – and is so on a purely scientific level.

To measure time, human beings took the rotation of our planet. The earth revolves upon itself and at the same time revolves around the sun. Starting from this fact, we constructed the day, the hour, the minute and the second. However, we now know that the earth is slowing down, that the speed of its rotation is diminishing by ten seconds every thirteen years. So days now are slightly longer than they used to be: good news for all those who are growing old!

If this tendency is maintained, then in fact days will be perceptibly longer for coming generations, and in the long term that will also have an effect on our climate.

So we know that this standard of time is not stable, and is constantly changing. People used to adjust their watches to the rotation of the earth, but now that no longer works; the earth has proved to be too capricious and we cannot count on it: its movement is too irregular. So our scientists have had to discover another standard. First they used atomic clocks, which work to an accuracy of a thousandth of a second. Quartz clocks are even more amazingly precise: their possible deviation is no more than a thousand billionth of a second a year.

The time of such clocks is based on the vibrations of an atom, in practice hydrogen, rubidium, or above all caesium. Starting from this, the thirteenth General Conference of Weights and Measures held in Paris in 1967 defined the second as 'the duration of 9,192,631,770 periods of emission between the two hyperfine levels of the basic state of the atom of caesium 133'. In other words, atomic time is

$$\frac{1}{9,192,631,770} = \text{TAI (Temps Atomique International)}.$$

Think of that next time you adjust your watch!

So according to scientists there are two quite different times:

I = TAI – Temps Atomique International
   International Atomic Time, which denotes the regular continuity of time with the utmost possible accuracy.

II = TU – Temps Universel
   Universal time, which relates to the speed with which the earth rotates.

There is no theoretical connection between TAI and TU. The difference between them varies in an unpredictable way and can only be recognized on the basis of previous astronomical observations. It has been decided that the difference between TU and TAI amounts to zero on 1 January 1968. But from that point onwards, TU and TAI have lives of their own. Since then the speed of the earth's rotation has decreased, so the TU principle is moving further away from the TAI principle. By now the TU clock is over fifteen seconds slow, and the difference between the two clocks will go on increasing.

Perhaps you may not be very interested in all this. But it is important for you to know that the time in which the whole of our lives elapses is relative to a great many factors.

Now having discovered that our objective time is relative to the rotation of the earth and even to the vibration of atoms, it has to be added that this time is also relative to space and to speed.

This was the great discovery made by Einstein, after extremely complicated calculations and years of reflection at his desk. In this way he was able to establish a rigorous relationship between time and speed which he expressed in his famous theory of relativity.

However, scientists, who tend to be convinced only by observation, wanted to try an experiment to test this theoretical relationship between time and speed. So on Tuesday, 5 October 1971, two American scientists boarded two Boeing 747s for one of the most interesting flights ever undertaken for the purposes of scientific research. Their aim was to test Einstein's theory of relativity in practice.

Each of them had with him an astronomical clock, weighing thirty kilos and costing $60,000, precise to a billionth of a second. It was Einstein's theory that if you fly two clocks round the earth, in one plane anti-clockwise and in another plane clockwise, while to begin with they will both tell the same time, after a few revolutions a difference will develop between them, and both will differ from a third clock, the control clock, on earth. The clock which goes round the earth clockwise will go slow, and the one which goes round the earth anti-clockwise will go fast. That would seem natural because of the direction in which the earth rotates: one clock is going against the movement of the earth and the other is following it.

But how did the experiment turn out? The clocks which were taken on the planes showed a difference of 300 billionths of a second from the control clock in the laboratory, and the speed at which they had been flown was far, far below the speed of light.

So this new experiment confirmed the idea that time goes more quickly on earth than in space. In that case astronauts who returned from what in earthly terms was a very long interplanetary flight would then logically have to be substantially younger than the families which they had left behind. A father could return younger than his own child or grandchild.

An even more conceivable experiment could be carried out with cats. Suppose one left three kittens to develop naturally and put the fourth into a rocket and fired that off into the universe at a speed approaching that of light. After a year of earthly time the little kitten would return more or less unchanged, while the other kittens who had grown up on earth would have become cats.

This theory has not been tested with cats, but it has been tested with inanimate objects and found to be true. Nowadays the majority of scientists believe it, and the duration of the life of our future astronauts will be quite different from what it is under present conditions. Suppose that I embarked in a spacecraft to explore space for the course of the further twenty or thirty years that I might expect to live. The amount of space that I might cover in this period of time would be ridiculously small compared with the dimensions of the universe: the polar star is forty light years away and the limits of our galaxy are around ten thousand light years away... But scientists encourage me and tell me that I shall live much longer in space. In space, the thirty years that I suppose to be my last would amount to sixty, a hundred or a thousand earth-years. In other words, the duration of my life would be relative to the speed at which my spaceship moved through the universe.

I expect that you have heard of the famous experiment of Langevin's train. Langevin's imaginary traveller gets on an astronomical train, the 'Einstein train'. It is five million kilometres long, goes in a straight line, and has a speed of 240,000 kilometres a second. There are two stations on this straight line, a distance of 864 million kilometres apart. Theoretically, the Einstein train takes an hour to cover this distance. The passenger will be amazed to see that when he arrives, his watch is slow compared with the station clock. But the fact of the matter is that it is not his watch which is slow, but the station clock which is fast. What would have been one hour for someone standing on the station is only one hour minus x for the passenger. This is an enormous challenge to ordinary common sense, but it can be demonstrated by precise mathematical calculations. The knowledge that even the physical concept of time is relative is in fact staggering.

I now want to demonstrate this relativity of time in the sphere of our personal life. The Bible tells us of people who live to be 900 years old. Fine, though I do not know whether I would want to live so long. We would do better to ask about the meaning of our life than about its duration. What is the meaning of a long life of 100 or 900 years or of just a short one of twenty years? The biological rhythm of a human body and the movement of a clock are by no means one and the same, which is why the sense of time of a child of eight is very different from that of a man or woman of eighty. For the child, whose small organism is growing rapidly, an hour is a very long time, since within this period an enormous amount is experienced and assimilated, and in the process of this the child goes through a wide range of the most varied reactions and emotions. I remember my earliest schooldays and the eternity of some of the lessons: the boredom was often torture; I kept looking at my watch and it just would not move. Why? I think that it was because my biological rhythm was going ten times faster than the watch and what went on in school. But the old man or woman, whose biological rhythm seems to go ten times slower than the ticking of a watch, has the impression that the hours are rushing by, so that an hour amounts to virtually nothing.

We encounter the same phenomenon in hibernation. You may well have seen the film *2001 A Space Odyssey*. In it we are shown enormous blocks of ice, at the heart of which we can recognize human bodies, deep-frozen men and women. They are carried through space in a spaceship, to be unfrozen again on earth after a certain number of years travelling. It will then prove that these people have hardly grown any older, since the hibernation has slowed down their biological rhythm, because the body needs only a minimal amount of energy to keep it alive in such circumstances.

Here's an example from everyday experience. If I have breakfast at eight in the morning, I am hungry again by lunchtime. Why? Because I have burned up and consumed the energy provided by my breakfast during my morning's activity. But in the morning I am not usually very hungry, although it is twelve hours since I had supper. That is because the biological rhythm of the body has been slowed down considerably by my sleep. Hibernation works on basically the same principle as sleep. The body temperature is reduced to such a degree that the pulse-rate falls from eighty beats a minute to one every five minutes or even one every twenty-four hours. In these conditions the body consumes hardly any energy and can subsist for a very long time without sleep. We have long been aware of this from the practice of many animals – we call it winter sleep, hibernation. Marmots, for example, gather in groups underground, fill up the space with dry grass, and curl up in their skins to preserve some warmth. Then they go to sleep for up to nine months without food or liquid. In principle the same thing is possible for human beings.

In America there are already commercial companies which offer their clients an extended life through hibernation. For a few million dollars they can be deep-frozen for a period of from a few decades to perhaps several hundred years. Suppose I am fifty and I say that I would like to know what is happening on earth in the year 2090. I go to one of these companies in America and say, 'hibernate me for a century'. After paying the bill, I am put in a glass case, stored in a deep freeze and have a good long sleep. In 2090 I am taken out, unfrozen, tapped on the shoulder and told, 'There you are, 2090!' I should only be fifty-one, since during the century I would have aged only one year. I would be able to see what is happening in the twenty-first century and continue my normal life. Apparently at this moment there are deep-frozen human bodies resting peacefully in the store-cupboards of these businesses.

In fact my twenty-four-hour biological rhythm is inscribed on my organism, and the same is true of plants and animals. How is it that when you decide to wake up at 6 a.m. and set your alarm clock for that time, you often wake up two minutes beforehand? It is because you have an internal organic clock which measures time almost as rigorously as a mechanical clock. Researchers have carried out experiments with life in total darkness, expecting this to produce a different rhythm from our twenty-four-hour one. They lived in caves in total darkness, without clocks. For several weeks they would not have been able to tell whether it was day or night in the world, and yet they lived the quite normal human twenty-four-hour rhythm of sleeping, waking and taking food. This rhythm determines our organism, and it is inadvisable to disturb it.

Air hostesses, who are continually subject to time changes between Tokyo, New York and Paris, have day and night constantly turned upside down. But since their body clocks function by a normal twenty-four-hour rhythm, these continual changes risk disturbing their bodies in a dangerous way.

One of the reasons for the imbalances nowadays is that there is no longer day or night. During the day people are shut up in dark offices and the night is bathed in light and neon. People go to bed at four in the morning and get up at eleven: night is day and day is night. There is respect neither for biological rhythm nor for the succession of day and night. That could be serious. I am not saying that we should all go to bed at sunset like birds or hens, but I think that there is a certain rhythm that we should respect, and that normally we should get up when the sun rises. That is programmed into our organism.

A further example of the relativity of time of which some of you may be aware ought to be mentioned here. We have the impression that the two thousand years which have elapsed since the birth of Christ is a considerable time. In fact, if we put this period in the total history of the universe, we can see that these two thousand years amount to virtually nothing.

To get some idea, we might reduce the thirteen billion years for which the universe seems to have existed to a calendar year of 365 days. On that scale, life will have appeared at the beginning of October. Up to that point the universe was lifeless: nothing but minerals, pure matter. At the beginning of October, somewhere, at the bottom of a marsh, bacteria formed: that was the appearance of life. On 22 December, vertebrates and the nervous system emerged. On 29 December, at around four in the afternoon, mammals appeared, i.e. animals which carry their young within their bodies rather than laying eggs. And on 31 December, at around 9.20 in the evening, human beings appeared! So human beings appeared on earth only just over two hours ago, in comparison with all the former periods of the history of the universe.

And on 31 December, at 11.59 and 55 seconds, Jesus was born. So the two thousand years between Jesus and ourselves amount to no more than just five seconds in a history of the universe totalling 365 days. Therefore when we are told that Christ ushers in the end of time, we can understand that in terms of what I have just said.

Everything that I have summarized here relativizes our conception of time to an enormous degree. And does not the Bible tell us that for God 'a thousand years are as a day' (II Peter 3.8)? It is a phrase which was already used in the Psalms (90.4).

Something else changes the usual picture of time that we have: the use of drugs, which puts people in an exceptional state, in a world without time. A young woman on drugs has told of her experience in a very interesting autobiography entitled *Blue Grass*. In it she says:

I remember having read somewhere that a thousand years of human life were only a second for the Lord, and I told myself that I had at last found the solution. I was there living my life on the usual time-scale, and at the same time living the life of thousands of human beings in the space of an hour.

I have made the same point in my lectures on death. The last moment in a human life is a total moment, a moment in which all that one has gone through and experienced comes before one and is concentrated at one point. At this point the totality of our personal experience will be summed up, and in the light of this comprehensive view we shall make what Ladislas Boros has called 'the final choice', the last important human decision on which eternal life will depend.

So the value of time is related to the intensity with which we live it. What does it mean to live thirty years, sixty years, ninety years? To talk like that says nothing either about the value of this life or about its true duration.

Time passes at a speed relative to the intensity of the life that is lived and the quality of life that is experienced. Perhaps there are people of ninety who in fact have really lived for only three years of their lives. Why? Because their lives were so empty, so hollow, so inconsistent that they amounted to only a few days or years. These people have not lived; they have just lasted. What is the point of a life which just goes on and on like this over ninety years?

People talk a lot nowadays about living a long life, and scientists and doctors are trying to prolong human life as much a possible. But what is the point of adding years to years if they are all as empty as the ones which precede them, if they have no content? In Arabic there is a greeting, '*Allah yetawwel omrak*', 'May God prolong your life!' But I would not wish you a long life if that meant merely an extended life: I would wish you a life filled as much as possible with inner fulfilment. A few years lived out intensively can be more than a hundred useless, wasted years. It is not duration that makes life significant, but its quality.

I'm not interested in knowing how old you are, because I know old people who are as bright as twenty-year-olds and twenty-year-olds who act as though they were eighty. It is your heart which determines how old you are.

I would like to add some thoughts which I wrote down in Lebanon in 1962:

'It is not time that we lack, but heart.' Never say that you have no time. On the whole it is those who are busiest who can make time for yet more, and those who have more leisure-time who refuse to do something when one asks. What we lack is not time, but heart.

'True time is not the time of the clock or the calendar but the time of consciousness.' You may have four months vacation which are worth forty years because they provide such rich and intense experiences that you can live a whole life in a summer. For other people, these four months are worth less than four hours, because this time has been empty, sheer absence. True time is not the time of the clock or the calendar, but the time of consciousness.

'There are moments which are worth hours and hours which are not worth a moment.' In fact, the capacity to live the present moment intensely makes this moment an experience which infinitely surpasses its own limits.

'The concentration of time relates to an intensity of emotion, of life, of sensation and interest.' How is it that in certain courses the teacher has hardly begun to speak than three-quarters of an hour is already up, while in others the clock seems so reluctant to move forward? What's the reason? It is that time is a very relative concept and that it primarily relates to our interest in what is going on.

'Time that one feels passing is time lost.' 'You do not escape time by evasion, but by attention.' Some people try to 'kill time', as they say, and to do so they try to find ways of 'diverting themselves' in order to escape boredom. Quite apart from the fact that this is a criminal waste which dissipates precious capital and potential riches, it has to be added that the enterprise is vain and ineffective because the problem can be solved only by constructive work and purposeful and impassioned activity. It is when I concentrate all my attention on a task which captivates me that time passes and in a way is suppressed. We do not escape time by evasion but by attention.

'Love abolishes time.' The same goes for love. For lovers, time stands still and ceases to exist. One might think of the couple who spend a night in each other's arms, only to feel as the first rays of dawn appear that they have only been there a moment. The long night passes in the twinkling of an eye. By contrast, if while you are with your girlfriend or boyfriend you spend your time looking at your watch, you can be sure that the relationship is nearly over. The same goes for dreaming and playing: children at play lose all sense of time, and that is also true for us if we are concentrating on playing cards or chess. When we really get into a book or are caught up in work which interests us, we can even forget food and sleep. 'There is only one true time, that of love.'

The words which I used earlier, 'intensity of emotion, of life, of sensation and interest', all basically express one reality, that of love. The last function of time is without doubt to blossom and flourish in love, to suppress oneself in it. It is to this change that we are invited, and that is perhaps the ultimate meaning of our life.

I now want to end this chapter with a brief reflection on this change that is taking place in the notion of time today and on its psychological and spiritual repercussions for us.

In our day we are experiencing something like a concentration of time and a contraction of duration: a year today is worth a thousand at other times. I read recently that over the past decade more scientific discoveries have been made than during the whole period of human life on this earth. We are witnessing something like an acceleration of evolution: the motor of progress is under pressure, if not overloaded.

The course of time is accelerating by a geometric progression:

three billion years ago, life;
four million years ago, human beings;
two thousand years ago, Jesus Christ.

The speed of progress is accelerating similarly:

three million years ago the Stone Age;
ten thousand years ago the first civilization;
two hundred years ago the industrial age;
fifty years ago the beginning of the atomic age.

In the near future, the speed of ongoing changes to life may reach a critical point at which the direction changes. Perhaps that will give us a new perspective on things. And along with the acceleration of time goes another phenomenon, namely the contraction of space, and that is again something new. So on earth a process is taking place in which time and space are both becoming increasingly unreal.

When President Sadat of Egypt was shot, the news was immediately known all round the world and in a flash the heads of state had gathered in Cairo for the funeral. In France there is a new train, the TGV, which can go from Paris to Lyons in two hours. Concorde can cross the Atlantic in three and a half hours, and a satellite can circle the earth in an hour and a half. So the concentration of time is closely bound up with the contraction of space, and it seems that time and space belong together in solidarity. It is probably quite unavoidable that, seen as a whole, these phenomena have repercussions on each individual consciousness, causing a state of tension which is likely to increase.

People nowadays find in their bodies and their consciousnesses that everything is going much faster, and this causes tension. I spoke earlier of uncertainty and anxiety. This uncertainty and this anxiety are largely the result of the universal phenomenon of which I have just spoken, which has repercussions deep within the human heart. And if we are to be capable of taking such tension and living with it, we are asked for a true inner conversion, a radical change of being. Without this *sursum corda*, this raising ourselves up to higher things, we risk losing our souls and with them our humanity.

To return to where we started, I would like to stress once again that today the most urgent thing for us is to learn how to save our beings, to save our souls. Faced with this whirlwind which blows us so powerfully along its course, we must more than ever be ready deliberately to draw back, to look at things with a degree of detachment, so that we are not caught up in and torn apart by the mad rush. We must not heedlessly take part in this helter-skelter of our time, climb aboard the relentless carrousel of events, but find our place at its centre.

Here, from the centre, we can watch the movement of the world at the periphery without ourselves coming to grief. Rather than joining in with the world, we need more than ever to keep our hearts quiet and peaceful, to keep our minds calm and lucid, to keep our gazes clear and gentle, and to keep our souls as still as a mountain lake.

If we are to be capable of enduring this increasing tension in the world without dying from it, it is urgent for us to rediscover the inner peace which will allow us to dominate this movement without becoming its slaves or victims. That is not an escape from time or an evasion of the world, but an essential condition for acting in it in truth and depth and in breathing a spirit into it. More than ever we need calm, lucidity, meditation, contemplation and silence:

'What does it serve a man if he gains the whole world and loses his own soul?' (Luke 9.25).

2   The Depth of the Present

'If the moment is mine and I take heed of it,
then He is mine who made time and eternity'
(*Andreas Gryphius*)

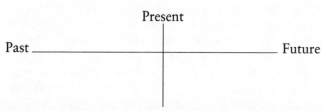

What is the present? Is it not just a simple point of contact between the past and the future, the zero point at which these two time-lines meet? But what is such a point, if not sheer nothingness? A point does not exist. In mathematics a point has no volume, no surface; it is nothing. When two straight lines meet, what is the consistency of their meeting point? It remains a mathematical abstraction, an idea, since it has no real existence. If it had a real existence, it would already be a line, a surface or a volume. But a point is neither a surface, a line or a volume; it is a point.

So if the present is only a point, it does not exist, because the past is advancing and the future is receding, the one occupying the space which the other leaves clear. When I say 'now', this 'now' has passed by the time I have stopped saying it and it already belongs to the past. If I try to catch the coming 'instant', at the moment when I catch it, it is already behind me. So the quest for the present is an endless pursuit of the intangible, the evanescent, which constantly escapes us. The past is no more, the future is not yet, but what is the present? Is it not the future, which is not yet and which is already here, becoming the past, in other words something which is no longer? Everything vanishes before our inner eye, and there is nothing but a void.

Georges Duhamel remarked: 'Between the future and memory,

[17

human beings have to come to grips with what they least possess, the present.'

So we have arrived at an utterly discouraging idea of the present, rather like the experience of someone walking east at sunset and trying to catch his shadow.

But let us look at things a bit more closely. Is the present really only this fleeting moment without existence, without significance? Is it a point which no one can grasp, since its nature is to dissolve, instantly and irrevocably? I said earlier that the present has no existence, no permanence, that it has no reality. Now I want to assert exactly the opposite. Only the present exists and there is nothing else. The present is the only reality and it is imperishable.

The present is imperishable because everything meets and crosses in it. In this sense it is distinct from the 'ephemeral' which is purely evanescent, totally without permanence. The present concentrates time in itself: past and future are resolved in it; the arrow of the future, far from pointing towards an indefinite tomorrow, falls into this 'now' in which everything happens and from which everything originates. The present is that reality which combines the past and the future and gives both of them meaning and value. Because the present concentrates time in itself, to some degree it is beyond the influence of time and belongs to the realm of eternity.

The temptation of many of us, however, is to flee the present and to take refuge cosily in 'the good old days'. The past can be so comforting; provide such a sense of security; we feel so at ease in what we have lived through, like being in a house we have lived in for a long time, that in our return to the past there is always the danger of evasion and a flight from the real world. Now the real world is the present, and nothing but that really exists for me.

People begin to grow old from the moment they close their eyes and take refuge in the past. For young people, the opposite is the case. Their temptation is not to escape the present for the past but to escape into a utopian, marvellous, miraculous future, somewhere on the horizon. This future is called 'tomorrow': tomorrow I will do..., tomorrow I will be..., tomorrow I could... Instead of engaging in today's struggle they risk living out their dreams of tomorrow and the day after tomorrow in their imagination.

Albert Camus commented: 'The greatest fidelity to the past is to give everything to the present.'

In other words, the past is the force which has shaped me and made me, and is now standing at the gateway of the present, where it presses and pushes with all its vigour to move me on further, to shape and to create, to create myself. With all that I have been and all that I have experienced, I am invited to do new things in this present which is given me. So the past exists, but as a power capable of constructing the present.

What I am talking about is therefore an invitation to live out the present in fullness. The word 'fullness' is a marvellous one. It expresses a density of existence in which one can steep oneself and feel filled, satiated, refreshed. We have to know how to dive into the present like a diver diving into the sea, completely and totally. We need to learn how to immerse ourselves with all our being in the here and now.

We have to tell ourselves that every moment of our lives is unique; the moment 'now' is unique. And this moment bears an absolutely unique message. The important thing for us is to seize this message. And this message is neither that of yesterday nor that of the day before yesterday, neither that of last week nor that of last year. Moreover, it is not that of tomorrow or the day after tomorrow or next year. It is that of now. The present moment brings me on a plate a hot, burning, absolutely new and original message which can enrich me infinitely. That is the sense in which I was speaking of fullness. 'Now' bears within it a fullness to which I need to open myself.

I must receive this magic of the passing moment as grace, pluck it like a fruit, take it in both hands and bite it with my teeth to taste and savour it. I do that by an act of concentrated attention: attention to the fleeting moment. To the degree to which I am capable of this act, the most trivial event can leave a deep mark on me and become a true existential experience.

In fact I truly remember only those acts which I experienced intently with my whole being – on such a day, at such a time, in such a place, with such a person I experienced something unique and unforgettable, which was a point of reference for the rest of my life.

Why was that? Because between me and what I experienced there was action and reaction. Because I experienced and savoured this apparently trivial event in the depth of the present. We need to ask ourselves whether we are really present in our lives, whether we are really taking part in the events that we are experiencing.

Do we pass by the real? Do we not often just run parallel to a certain number of the realities which surround us, as strangers and distracted spectators of the world in which we live, a world which does not really get to us?

Here I would like to commend something which in religious terminology is called 'self-examination'. I know that some of you will raise your eyebrows at that unattractive word, which evokes a morbid obsession with sin and a feeling of guilt towards it. However, self-examination is not what you think. Before being a meticulous review of all the mistakes you have made during the day, all your follies, it is first of all a recollection of the moments of grace which you have experienced. For me it is recollection in depth of what has been a unique and singular experience, one which has marked me and transformed me. Only such experiences allow me really to grow and develop. It is to the degree that my being has some contact with reality, action and reaction, that it develops.

Self-examination is the time when I pay attention to those important experiences which have made me grow, to those moments of the present from which I draw all the substance and all the sap, and which because of that form 'moments of grace'. A moment of grace is an ecstatic moment in which I decentre myself completely and plunge into a reality which fascinates, absorbs and fills me. It is a moment in which I open myself to the Spirit and let it invade me.

Self-examination consists in identifying these moments of grace, in finding in my day those 'touches of the Spirit', and at the same time in noting the moments when I became hardened and shut in on myself, when I was absent-minded or distracted, when I passed reality and other people by without wanting to get more deeply into them. Here the Spirit could not reach me because I was not there; I was not accessible to its breath and its grace. For grace is given to us in the present, in the action by which we are present, and make ourselves present to others and to the world. By opening us up to all that is around us, this act of presence also opens us up to grace.

Seen from this perspective, self-examination then takes on an extraordinary richness. It forms the harvest of the day, the moment when we gather those precious moments of fullness which we experienced during the day, to taste and savour them in a mood of thanksgiving.

The mistake of those who calculate time mathematically is to forget that every moment is unique, so that moments cannot be added together one by one. When I say 'one hour, two hours, three hours, four hours', it is as if the first, second, third and fourth hours were all alike. But they are not. These hours are quite different from one another. To the degree that at a precise moment I have had a quite unique experience, this hour infinitely surpasses the concept of sixty minutes and takes on quite a different density and dimension, beause I have experienced something which I did not experience in the other three hours, and this something cannot be compared with all the rest.

The mathematical measuring of time is quite a relative matter. I am not going to return to it, because I spoke of it at length in the first chapter. However, now we can see how the two themes are connected.

What is true on the physical level is also true on the psychological and spiritual levels. Time is relative to the quality and the intensity with which I live out the present moment. The French poetess Countess de Noailles wrote, 'We shall never be able to call our souls our own more than we can this evening.' That's a splendid remark! She thought that the evening she was spending with a friend was unrepeatable. They both experienced it so deeply that they already found it quite incomparable. And I am sure that each of us has had this personal experience in our lives, on a particular day and in a particular place.

If we really enter into this perspective, then we make the marvellous discovery that each moment everything is new. And nothing is old. The old does not exist. The old exists only for those who make themselves old, who want to be old. Everything is new each moment for those who have young hearts. This reminds me of a fine verse by Mallarmé: 'Today is virgin-fresh and beautiful.'

Today is the reality which is born at this moment as it were from nothing, fresh as the dew at the first moment of creation.

Children live in this wonderful world of incessant amazement. Children experience only the present. But as we grow up, we lose this good fortune and look nervously forwards and backwards – and do only that. By contrast, children live only in the present moment. When they play, they are caught up in their games, lost in them. When you tell them a story, there they are, mouth open, wide-eyed, lapping up the story, thinking of nothing else, all else forgotten. When they go to sleep, they are tranquil and restful: 'Sweet dreams,' we say. But when *we* go to bed, we wonder 'What have I done? What have I not done? What am I going to do tomorrow? What should I have done today?' And we get insomnia.

We need to react against what we call habit, and that includes dull everyday repetition. I can make my stereotyped actions new each time if I can turn them into something unique and original.

You may say to me, 'But I cook every day.' 'Yes.' 'I go to the office every day.' 'Yes.' 'So?' 'Today can be very different from yesterday.' 'But it's the same cooking, the same office.' 'Not necessarily.'

'Why?'

'Because you are no longer the same. You are different from yesterday, and by the same token your cooking, your office are also different. The people you will meet today will also have changed; they are not the same as they were yesterday and the day before.'

If I am capable of living out this daily newness, everything will take on an inner light and a new appearance every day. It's a question of soul, a question of inner attitude; it's a question of being young at heart. Keep your heart young, and your life will be new each day. Some people find their life terrifyingly monotonous: yesterday, today, tomorrow; office, travel, sleep. It's all a matter of the attitude with which we approach things. We can restore and refresh ourselves by thinking positively, by curiosity, by enthusiasm. Every day can be something special.

Our discouragement and feeling that everyday life is intolerable comes about above all because we are always dealing with the same people: the husband with his wife, the wife with her husband, children with their parents, parents with their children, teachers with their pupils, employers with their employees, and so on. And so we no longer really see one another. Why is that? It's because we think that we have discovered husband or wife, pupils or employees. A husband may think he knows his wife inside out, that he has squeezed her like a lemon so that there is nothing left but skin and pips. There's no more to get out of her. But we never get to the end of other people. We never get to the end of our husbands, wives, children, friends, colleagues at work. Human beings have inexhaustible depths, and if someone seems to me always to be the same, it is because I have not yet discovered his or her real depths. What we need to do is look again, change the way in which we look at one another.

One day I had this experience with someone who had been living next to me for years. I said to myself, 'Look, you really don't know him.' 'What? I know him very well.' 'No you don't. Look at him today as though you were meeting him for the first time.' So that day I did, and something quite essential dawned on me, something very important that I had not yet discovered about this person I thought I knew.

What I have said about meeting other people I could equally well say about getting to know myself. I think I know myself. But in fact I scarcely do at all. The essentials escape me. So there are some people who have had too much of themselves, who feel tired of themselves, who are discouraged, like the prophet Elijah who collapsed under a tree and said, 'It is enough, Lord. Now take away my life' (I Kings 19.4). That was the point at which God, with a morsel of bread and some water, gave him new strength which enabled him to go for forty days and forty nights to the mountain of God.

There are people who think that they have exhausted what they are. They have to be told, 'Look deep within yourself, and at the depth of your being you will discover new strength, unsuspected riches.'

Look at other people, look at yourselves, look at your country. When we look at our country we may well be deeply pessimistic, hopelessly disappointed. And very many people may be unable to believe in a revival, believe that things can get any better. A negative past can often make us react to the present in an excessively negative way, write causes and people off and not give them a chance. So we need to tear down walls, to look for a new being and allow it to emerge.

Great educators or great spiritual figures are those who release people from their past, put them in the present, and from that position show them a new perspective on the future. These are the people who believe that life can begin again and who create confidence in others. 'Today your life is beginning again; today everything is new and you can make a new start. Do you believe that?' 'Yes, I do.' 'Your past no longer exists. I have forgotten it. You forget it. Your life begins now. Now. Do you believe that?' 'Yes, I believe it.' That is rebirth and resurrection and radical transformation.

That is what is called a conversion, i.e., according to the etymology of the word, a 180-degree turn in which instead of looking backwards a person suddenly looks forwards, and as a result becomes a completely new being. Psychology all too often encloses people in their past, their childhood, their education, their instincts, their heredity, their sub-conscious, and this past weighs so heavily on the present that people become its slaves and its prisoners. This is where faith comes in, stronger and more true than any psychoanalysis: the word of faith which says to people, 'You are not a prisoner of your past or of your subconscious or of your heredity or of your education or of anything that you have experienced so far. And today, now, your life is beginning.'

That is resurrection faith. Not a future resurrection at the end of history, in a more or less uncertain future, but resurrection 'today, here and now'. That is the good news, the joyful news, the great news of the gospel:

The lame walk, the deaf hear, the blind see, the dead are raised (Matthew 11.2-15; Luke 7.22).

Arise, take up your bed and walk (Mark 2.9).

Lazarus, come forth (John 11.43).

That is the liberating word of Christ which we have to take account of and repeat after him to all those lying around us, dead tired, the victims of their past. Grace is offered to us, here and now, to begin our lives all over again.

When St Augustine discovered God in his life he exclaimed, 'What beauty, existing from eternity yet always new!'

Our God is the God who is new each day and who renews men and women each day, giving them new strength and new youth. 'I will go to the altar of God, the God of my joy and gladness,' runs Psalm 42, which began the old Latin Mass.

Another idea which I want to go into more deeply is that of contemplation, because there is a close relationship between the present and contemplation. Contemplation is the capacity to steep ourselves in the present, to look at the world and others in an entirely open way, so freely and disinterestedly that it can easily penetrate to the heart of reality.

The difference between contemplation and action is that in action, as soon as I see anything, I say, 'What's that for? What can I do with it? How can I use it? How much does it cost? Where does it come from?' This is a utilitarian and pragmatic attitude, based on intelligence.

By contrast, contemplation does not seek to know the use of something, what I can do with it, the profit I will gain from it, but is content to look on it with tenderness and love, and that creates the possibility of penetrating slowly right into its depths. Contemplation is steeped in the present; it is a welcoming of being into itself without any afterthoughts, the love of the other simply for the other's sake.

Our relations with one another are often purely utilitarian: 'Good morning, sir. What are you doing? Where are you working? Can I have your visiting card?...' And I make a note in my book: 'This man works in such and such a company; one day he may be able to help me out.' You may smile, but that's what happens. Our relationships with one another are often centred on interest and profit. We ask ourselves how we can exploit or make use of a particular person. And that can be true even when we gather together in church meetings.

Quite gratuitous, disinterested encounters, meetings with another person just for that person's sake, are very rare. 'I'm interested in you just for your own sake, because I enjoy your company.'

This attitude develops in us an interest in other people: concern for other people, attention to other people. And that's what contemplation is.

Contemplation is not necessarily a matter of thinking of God. Contemplation is a matter of immersing ourselves in the heart of reality. And to anyone who is capable of taking the plunge, reality suddenly unveils itself, presents itself in its truth, reveals its truth. But this revelation is possible only if our gaze is pure enough to penetrate this secret sanctuary without violating it or seeking to possess it.

Contemplation is an attitude of mind which does not need either a monastery or a desert to be practised in. We can develop this contemplative gaze which penetrates to the heart of reality in order to reach its soul in the midst of our ordinary everyday life. Contemplation is the capacity to live out the present fully.

John Dewey, the great American educational theorist, stressed the sovereign importance of experience in education. 'Only living experience shapes and determines a child's development.' In Egypt, almost all education is based on memory and the effort of memorizing. Instead of letting pupils have experiences, teachers make them learn by heart the results of the experiments of others. Now Dewey tells us that anything that children have not worked out for themselves is nothing, pure zero. It does not leave any mark on them and slides off them like water off a duck's back. At the end of the child's education we have an empty, dried-up being, who has learnt a good deal, but whose heart has remained empty because he or she has experienced nothing, felt nothing, experimented with nothing. That is why so many schools leave so little mark on children: their real life is elsewhere.

John Dewey says to us: 'Each of us must think back and ask ourselves what has become of all the knowledge that we accumulated during our years at college.' What did you learn during your years at school? Dewey went on to ask: 'Why are we obliged to relearn everything afterwards? Because this teaching was not based on an immediate and actual experience of reality, but on notions aimed at preparing for experiences to come.'

At school we may be prepared for future experiences, but we may not have present experiences. But the only thing that counts is an intense present experience. Dewey again comments:

> It is at the moment when one has an experience that one derives from it all that is possible to retain. If, by contrast, we sacrifice the present for the future, as happens in traditional schools, we ruin everything and this supposed preparation for the future is a sheer waste of time.

> We always live in the present moment and not in any other, and it is only by deriving the maximum from this passing moment that we really prepare ouselves for the future. Living the experience of the present moment to the full is the only thing that matters for our future formation.

Let me add something from my own experience. If you want to give a lecture, do not think about what you are going to say when you give the lecture, but try, rather, to feel intensely what you want to say, to live out the subject in depth to the point of being literally possessed by it. You may then be sure that the lecture will go well. Why? Because the lecture will become a living spring, deriving from a real experience. That is why the Lord said to us, 'Take no thought for the morrow; the morrow will take thought for itself' (Matt.6.34).

Live the present to the full! Live out the moment! Immerse

yourself in experience! That is the best guarantee for your preparation for tomorrow.

Making the substance of the present a personal experience by steeping oneself deeply in it is the best guarantee for whatever is to come. You may perhaps have read the famous novel by Nikos Kazantzakis, *Zorba the Greek*. It made a great impression on me and I quote it often, because I find the figure of Zorba quite extraordinary; for me he is a unique figure in world literature. This is what he says:

> I've stopped thinking all the time of what happened yesterday. And stopped asking myself what's going to happen tomorrow. What happens today, this minute, is what I care about. I say, 'What are you doing at this moment, Zorba?' 'I'm sleeping.' 'Well, sleep well.' 'What are you doing at this moment, Zorba?' 'I'm working.' 'Well, work well.' 'What are you doing at this moment, Zorba?' 'I'm kissing a woman.' 'OK, kiss her well, Zorba! And forget all the rest while you're doing it; there's nothing else on earth, only you and her. Get on with it!'

And later:

> When she, Bouboulina, was alive, you know, no one had ever given her so much pleasure as I did – old rag-and-bone Zorba. Do you want to know why? Because anyone else in the world, while they were kissing her, kept thinking about their fleets, or the king of Crete, or their stripes and decorations, or their wives. But I used to forget everything else, and she knew that, the old trollop. And let me tell you this, my learned friend – there's no greater pleasure for a woman than that.

Ask yourself the same questions as old Zorba did and live in the moment. Follow his example, his complete interest and genius in every form of work and occupation.

Now I want to develop some important ideas of the German philosopher Martin Heidegger, for he too stresses the unique value of the present as the context of action. For Heidegger, the present is presence, presence in the world. 'Man is a being in the world, but he is not in it like a coat in a cupboard.'

We are beings who act; we are in an interrupted process of action and reaction with our world. Science, too, tells us that every reality in the world, even matter, is in action and reaction with the rest of the universe, if only on the basis of universal attraction, the law of gravity. A piece of chalk that I hold in my hand, which evidently does not have the least thing in common with a table, in reality has a good deal to do with one. Everything is related and akin to everything else, and is in interaction with it: you as a person and the Eiffel tower or the pyramid of Cheops are related to this piece of chalk in my hand. In a most mysterious way the part is bound up with the whole, what we call the universe. There is even a real relationship of action and reaction between this chalk and the remotest star, for 'to be' means 'to be active': all being is active.

That is true to the greatest extent of human beings, who are never purely passive. Human beings, Heidegger says, are not just a part of this world but above all are in it. And being in the world means being constrained to act, to take an attitude, to be responsible for one's existence and the possibilities for which one opts. The future is a matter of coming to oneself. The future is the projection of our possibilities of realizing ourselves from what we are, i.e. from our past. At the beginning of my project I take on my past and project it on my future as a flow of energy. My project is what I already bear within myself, what I really am, and what one day will be realized. Then I shall have 'come to myself', I shall have 'become myself'. So, strictly speaking, the present is my birth; it is the moment at which I bring myself to birth, the moment in which the project takes shape and comes to maturity. Therefore in the end neither the past nor the future count, but only this germ of the self in me, which is the project of my life and which will develop slowly through successive acts of presence.

So past, present and future, these three temporal spheres, are simply the development of the depth of my being and the realization of the decisive plan of my life. Heidegger says that time is simply the 'development of a project in space', the realization of a plan. Time as a task! These thoughts fit very well with a splendid passage from the biblical book of Ecclesiastes, of which I am very fond:

There is a time for every matter under heaven:
a time to be born, and a time to die;
a time to plant, and a time to pluck up what is planted;
a time to kill, and a time to heal;
a time to break down, and a time to build up;

a time to weep, and a time to laugh;
a time to mourn, and a time to dance;
a time to cast away stones, and a time to gather stones together;
a time to embrace, and a time to refrain from embracing;
a time to seek, and a time to lose;
a time to keep, and a time to cast away;
a time to rend, and a time to sew;
a time to keep silence, and a time to speak;
a time to love, and a time to hate;
a time for war, and a time for peace.
What gain has the worker from his toil?
 I have seen the business that God has given to the sons of men to be busy with. He has made everything appropriate to its time; also he has put eternity into man's mind, yet so that he cannot find out what God has done from the beginning to the end (Ecclesiastes 3.1-11).

Because there is a time for everything, immerse yourself in the present, and do completely what you are doing, with all your heart.
 Another idea of Heidegger's is the relationship which he establishes between the present and presence. There is no present in itself, but only present for a presence. It is my presence and your presence here which give the present its substance. This view of Heidegger's about time is resolutely personalist. There is no time without presence, and it is the person who incarnates the present, by being capable of being present to himself or herself and to reality. There is no present in itself, but there is a presence or presences in presence.
 I would now like to say something about three modes of presence:
 1. Being present to ourselves;
 2. Being present to the world;
 3. Being present to our fellow human beings.
 To be present to ourselves, which is something on which we have already reflected at length, is to refuse to escape into the past or into the present, and instead to enter into the present moment, to reflect on oneself, to gather oneself together. But modern men and women find it extremely difficult to live out this act of presence in this way. The characteristic feature of our age is the discontent, the anxiety that we meet in ourselves; we escape from ourselves.

Everybody complains about the noise, but what do we do when we are given a moment of peace and quiet, when we can be alone? We rush to the radio, the video, the television - or to the telephone, so that we can fill our solitude with sound and pictures. We suffer under the stress of events, but when we are by ourselves we bring this stress upon ourselves yet again by means of the television, in a more concentrated and louder form. We flee from our own presence, which is tangible in the stillness; we feel anxious about being alone with our selves and looking at our own image face to face.

How difficult it is to devote ourselves to prayer and meditation! I know some young people in a meditation group who have been trying to spend half an hour each day in silent prayer. If you ask them how easy it is, they will tell you that it is very difficult. Nevertheless, out of experience they recommend others not to turn silence into emptiness, which has to be filled at any price. Put your book aside and turn off the music. Sink into yourself. Only if you do this will the most important things be revealed to you and will you see the source in which you will find your origins. Those who are capable of being present to themselves in this way in prayer will find that in everything they do and say later, they will achieve a power which is almost limitless. Their language can become light and fire, and all their activity will prove effective. Why? Because they have immersed themselves in their being there; they have concentrated their thought, breathing, speech, action and being; and this concentrated power of being releases energy, so that their words and actions become amazing powerful.

A saint is a person who has found the unity of his or her being and who radiates and becomes effective from this focal point. His or her gaze penetrates others and moves them deeply; his or her words can quite simply move mountains, change society, help to renew our world. But the majority of us live in quite the opposite way; we prefer dispersion, distraction, which means that we apply only five or ten per cent of our true being to what we are doing and saying. That is why our action is often so superficial and ineffective.

There are techniques borrowed from Yoga or Zen, based on bodily feelings, to remedy this state. If you feel that your mind is wandering all over the place and is running off in all directions, turning to memories or plans; if you feel that a whirlwind is carrying you far away from the present in its spiral, become aware of your body again.

My body, my arms, my legs. Look, I have two arms. I have just seen them. I wasn't aware of them until just now and I can feel them resting on the table. I can feel my body resting on a chair, my legs on the carpet. I brush my hand over my face and I suddenly discover that I have a forehead, cheeks, a nose, ears. Little by little I feel a sensation of calmness and my mind slowly reintegrates my body and brings me back to myself. It's simple and very effective. Try the exercise for yourself, and you will see. Whole books have been written about it. I find particularly interesting the Vittoz method, which is based on 'bodily sensation'; it's a really good therapy for anxiety.

The phrase 'being beside ourselves' conveys the same sort of thing. We feel alienated from ourselves. And if we are going to come to ourselves again, we have to get ourselves under control. That means first of all controlling our bodies. Modern men and women can lose themselves, no longer be in full possession of their bodies, their senses; often they don't know one which way to lie to go to sleep. 'So many demands are made on me that I no longer know who I am.' No, for there is a time for everything, as we heard from the Bible, a time also for stillness and absorption – our fuel tank.

So the first priority is for us to be present to ourselves; this is our experience of our own presence. Secondly, we must be present to others, present in the world. It is not enough for us deliberately to make contact only with our own bodies, as we are taught by the methods I have mentioned; it is equally important to be in contact with our environment, which means constructing it and constantly developing it. We should become increasingly attentive to the details of the things and the beings around us, even to those things which seem insignificant, since nothing is without significance. We have to see everything and take it in. That will make our present ever richer and more precious, and we shall make contact with the reality of being.

We have plenty of time for this approach in our everyday life. If you are waiting for a bus or a train or a plane which is late and you are becoming edgy, look carefully at the people around you. Look at the cut of their clothes, the colour of their hair and the hairstyles, whether a man has a moustache, and so on. You may say that that doesn't interest you. In which case I must tell you that it should interest you, and that it is very important at this particular moment to know whether a certain person has a moustache or not.

If you do this, you will suddenly feel a great calm sweep over you and you may find something else in view, like a beautiful tree spreading its branches and saying to you 'admire me'. Or there might be a young woman a little further off with a certain air about her as she walks which says 'admire me'. You will find deep inside you a profound peace as you discover the reality that you are trying to escape. And then when what you have been waiting for actually arrives, it will be a pleasant surprise.

I recently had just this kind of experience. I had to celebrate mass at the Jesuit house at six and it was already twenty past. I couldn't find a taxi or a bus and I had to walk quite a distance from the central station to take a tram. Normally I would have been seething as I sat there in the tram, telling myself that there were fifteen people waiting for the mass. But at that point I said to myself, 'What's the point of sitting in your tram seething?', so I began to look at the people and the things around me. At one point I noticed that the tram station had not changed for forty-five or fifty years, since I was a child. I watched the stationmaster blowing his big whistle, but the tram didn't move. I smiled. Finally it set off, but it went very slowly and I said to myself, 'Just think of it – a tram that goes slowly!', and I smiled. Then I looked at the students getting on and strap-hanging. It all made me very calm.

I arrived at the mass thirty-five minutes late. But even if I had been in a bad temper, I would still have arrived at the mass thirty-five minutes late. Nervousness, excitement, anxiety often make us lose precious energy which we are just squandering. By living in the present, we concentrate all our potentialities, all our strength, all our energies, and exploit them to the full. There is a deep wisdom here.

This attention to concrete, ordinary reality can help us to make some extraordinary discoveries. We may notice with amazement that things are more beautiful and more interesting than we had thought. The artist sees that, and by concentrating on the most ordinary things can discover in them a hidden beauty which escapes us.

You will know about Van Gogh and his famous picture of the basket chair. Van Gogh turned this chair, which none of us would dare to offer to a guest, into a masterpiece. How did he do it? He knew how to look at it with love, knew how to look at it in a certain way, and this chair suddenly became beautiful. For most of us, 'beautiful' means sophisticated, ornate, gilded, decorated. People make frightful sitting rooms with gilding and imitation Aubusson tapestries and artificial bronzes, and we say, 'How beautiful!'

There are those who can only admire museum-pieces. They rush to Florence to see Michelangelo's David or to the Louvre to stare in admiration at the Mona Lisa, because someone has told them that these are beautiful and that they must be seen. But why go so far to admire beauty? Why go to museums to contemplate works of art? Your everyday world is bursting with works of art; they are all around you. Go to the seashore, sit on the sand and look at a small shell – it is far more beautiful than anything in the Vatican museum. Go into your garden, on to a balcony, into a park, and look at little plants beginning to grow, perhaps moving gently in the morning breeze. Is that not far more beautiful than anything in the Louvre?

This morning I spent a long time sitting on the concrete steps which lead down into the garden watching a cat surrounded by its six kittens. It was a real party. The kittens were literally laying siege to their mother: they were pouncing on her, nestling up to her, looking for milk from her, never leaving her alone for a moment, turning somersaults all round her. It was a marvellous sight, and I told myself that it was better than any of the films of Fellini or Rossellini. Why go to the cinema? Why switch on the television? I had much more.

The artist is the one who knows how to look; the mystic is the one who knows how to contemplate.

There are people who cannot appreciate their local countryside. They have to go to some remote place and discover the beauty of that. They have to consult their travel guides to know what has to be admired and when you have to say 'That's beautiful'. And they have to send postcards with exotic postmarks on them. But in virtually any place there is beauty for those who have eyes to see. The great photographers are not those who take pictures of magnificent countryside or majestic monuments. Anyone can do that. The real artist is the one who can make a masterpiece of a water jug, a rainy day, an old chair or an old dead tree. Why?

Because artists can open their eyes and their hearts to the most ordinary reality and find it extraordinary.

I have spoken about presence to the body, which is a matter of being present to ourselves. And I have also spoken of presence to the world, which is a matter of being present to reality. Now I have to talk about 'presence to the other', which I already mentioned earlier. This presence to the other is first of all 'presence of mind'.

Presence of mind is not just the capacity to mobilize our intellectual faculties to confront a critical situation, a fortuitous and unforeseen event. Quite apart from this practical aspect, presence of mind is presence to the other, the capacity to devote my whole attention to the person I encounter, to put myself wholly at his or her disposal.

If I am to do that, I have to convince myself that the person before me deserves my whole interest, my whole attention, my whole being. Some people are capable of this intense presence which makes one feel understood and known, makes oneself feel that what one is going to say has already been anticipated; such people are capable of vibrating to whatever one has to say: they can experience your drama or joy, drink in your words. You can feel that by their looks, their expressions, their actions and their words.

By contrast there are people who receive you in their office between their telephone, their diaries, their books and their files, and who say, 'Go on, I'm listening.' They will be listening to you while looking over the last report typed by their secretary, or the telephone book, or their eyes will stray to the morning paper. Oh yes, they're listening! When I find people like that I just get up and leave.

A great deal of misunderstanding and incomprehension, a great deal of tension, arises because we are not present to one another. We are there with our bodies but not with our hearts or our minds. We are there like wallpaper on a wall, or, to use Heidegger's phrase, like a coat in a cupboard.

'Being there' is not a physical act, but a spiritual act which involves our whole bodies. Being present to other people means giving them our time, our attention, our minds and our hearts. Presence of mind is also presence of the heart and of all our being. It can be seen in looks; it can be seen in smiles; it can be felt in handshakes or embraces. If that happens, there is true communication, action and reaction, and our presence to the other becomes an active and transforming presence.

I can spend two hours with a person without anything changing between us, because there has been no real encounter; we have spent two hours in parallel, as strangers to each other. By contrast, I need spend only five minutes with someone else to experience him or her with such attention, such intensity, such a 'presence of mind and heart', that these five minutes have truly been an 'event'. Something has happened because there has been real encounter. An encounter is not a juxtaposition of bodies but an osmosis of souls, a presence of minds, a fusion of hearts. All that happens only in the depth of the present as a place where things happen.

So only the present counts, for only it is true, only it exists. The present is the place of history; it is where history is made or unmade. It is here, today, now, that the destiny of the world is played out. What I say, what I do, here and now, changes the orientation of things, changes the course of history. Can you believe that? If you can, your present will take on an extraordinary density, fullness, force. Every instant, every moment, every present in my life means a change in universal history. It is not just elections that change our history. Nor is just discoveries like Einstein's theory of relativity that change history. Each one of my choices, each one of my moments, represents this turning point in universal history, since because of them history takes another course and by my action my present takes on fullness, seriousness, importance.

Once that has been understood, life changes meaning and becomes a passionate adventure. I once said to someone, 'Life is beautiful, isn't it?' He replied, 'No, it's not beautiful; it's fascinating.' The word beautiful is indeed inadequate to express the density of our existence. This existence is beyond beauty; rather, it is of another order, the tragic and sublime, and it is for me to make it so by living it to the full with all its intensity, by making each of my moments a present that I seize with both hands, an act of presence which immerses itself in the heart of reality.

Those who can understand that will help to transform the face of the earth.

3 Eternity at the Heart of Time

Jesus said to them, 'My Father is working still, and I am working' (*John 5.17*)

Eternity is a word which is largely out of favour at present. At best it is avoided or overlooked, and it can be totally denied. It is assumed that the category of the eternal is diametrically opposed to the temporal; it is thought that it is a kind of refuge, beyond the historical and physical world, into which people feel themselves born. Eternity can only mean 'somewhere else', in which many men and women take refuge, an opium of the people, a flight towards a distant and inaccessible unreality.

This criticism is certainly justified if applied to a particular conception of eternity, which tends to assimilate it to an atemporal, abstract order, to something which takes place up there beyond the clouds. There is no way, no communication, between the temporal and the eternal: in this view temporal and eternal represent two parallel lines which never meet. In order to attain the eternal, human beings have to abandon the temporal and escape this earth to find 'heaven'.

Another reason why eternity has fallen out of favour is that it has been conceived of as eternal duration, losing itself behind us in the darkness of time, from well before the creation of the world, and then reaching forward and disappearing before us into the mists of an indeterminate future, 'for ever and ever', as we say in our liturgies. That would make eternity a monotonous and boring eternalism which will never stop going on.

Moreover, such a conception suggests a phenomenon of repetition and morose tautology in which God indefinitely repeats himself *ad nauseam*, in incessant self-repetition, from one identical thing to the next. This is rather like the teaching of the fifth-century BC philosopher Parmenides: indefinite and immutable permanence of pure identity with itself.

The notion of eternity sometimes evokes a picture of God eternally contemplating himself with complacency and satisfaction, incessantly admiring himself as in a mirror: 'How beautiful I am! How great I am, how strong and powerful I am! I am God, always the same, always myself, for ever and ever.' And the saints in heaven, in beatific admiration, would have no function other than to praise, glorify and flatter this magnificent perfect God, beatifically enjoying the compliments that his heavenly court heaps on him.

I want us to try once and for all to get rid of this aberrant idea that we carry around in one form or another in our sub-conscious, and replace it with the true notion of eternity, which is the fullness of the present.

Here we pick up the theme of the previous chapter, which I would ask you to keep in mind as we go on.

When God reveals his identity in the book of Revelation, he says:

'I am the Alpha and Omega, the First and the Last, the Beginning and the End. I am he who is and was and is to come... the Living One' (Rev.1.8; 1.17; 22.13).

The eternity expressed by all these words can be summed up in the last of them: the Living One. God is 'the Living One'. That is how he already describes himself in the Old Testament. For Christians, the idea of the living God necessarily meets up with the idea of God as Trinity. God can only be living if he is Trinity. Why?

The gospel reveals to us that God is not pure identity with himself, but otherness and dialogue in the oneness of his divine essence. It is in the dialogue of the Father and the Son, in this outflowing of the Father into the Son, by the Spirit, that God is alive. God would not be a living God if he did not have within him this possibility of continually letting his living nature flow into that other self who is his Son, who lives within the divine heart, where the One is indivisible.

God is the living spring, the source of life. We have to say that before all creation, before any external expression of God's divine life, God is the source, the source in himself, of his very being. But without approaching the mystery of the Trinity, it is impossible to see how God could be the source in this way. The source of what? The source for what? It is equally difficult to see how God could be Love. Love of whom? Love for whom?

God is the source because God is Love, because God is Trinity. This eternal birth of God to himself in the mystery of the Trinity has as its cause the divine altruism which is at the same time an 'infinite capacity to love'. If God were not love, infinite love, God would not be eternal, God would not be sparkling life, would not be a source, a spring.

God is a living spring – and 'spring' is so rich, so profound a word that the church fathers often used it to talk of God. A spring is always new, always bubbling up, always flowing; it never exhausts itself, never grows old. So to say that God is a spring is to say that he is always young. The secret of God's youth is that God constantly empties himself – and constantly renews himself. God's being is not an indefinite repetition of himself, an eternal monotony, but a constant renewal. God never repeats himself. The being of God is always new. The face of God is always new. It is the interchange within the Trinity that is the secret of the perpetual being of God, making God an ever-flowing spring in the inexhaustible wonder of infinite ecstasy and self-giving.

The French writer Charles Péguy wrote a very beautiful poem which shows God contemplating his work at the beginning of creation, the brand-new world which has just emerged from his hands. God looks at it with wonder as the reflection of his own newness and his own youth:

And God himself, both young and eternal,
looked upon the flower of youth.
Like a father, he looked with paternal eye
on the world, gathered together like a humble village...

And God himself, both young and eternal,
looked upon time and age.
Like a father, he looked with paternal eye
on the world laid out like a beautiful village...

And God himself, both young and eternal,
looked upon time and space.
Calmly, gazing down with paternal affection,
he saw the image of God...

God is young and eternal. He is young because he is eternal, and he is eternal because he is young. There is a tendency to depict God as an old man with a beard, coming from the distant ages with all the weight of past centuries on his shoulders. But the reality is exactly the opposite. God, rather, should be represented as a child, as a baby, as a dawn, as a morning. It is not God who is old; we are old. God is eternal youth, the capacity for constant rejuvenation.

It was by discovering this eternal infancy of God that another French poet, Paul Claudel, was converted to Christianity one Christmas night. In this child in the manger, this newborn of Bethlehem, he discovered with wonder and amazement the most perfect expression of the very being of God, and his whole life was transformed as a result.

Christmas is the precise moment at which this eternal youth of God, this eternal childlikeness of God, irrupts into our world and establishes itself there for ever. In Jesus Christ, eternity has penetrated to the heart of time, the heart of history and the human heart.

In Jesus Christ a new and eternal covenant has been made between God and humankind. Note how Jesus brings together these two words, new and eternal.

We sometimes get the impression that in the incarnation God came to pay us a visit and then withdrew again into his heaven. The incarnation seems like a parenthesis which is opened at Christmas and closed again at the Ascension. God comes to live with us for thirty-three years and then says 'Good-bye' and returns home.

But that's not true. God has not come just to pay us a visit. Christ did not leave at Ascension; he simply disappeared from our eyes. For just before he 'went up to heaven', he told us, 'I am with you to the end of the world' (Matt.28.20). That is to indicate to us that his incarnation is a definitive act, an act by which he has inserted himself once for all at the heart of time and of history.

We say, 'The Lord came' (in the past) and we say 'The Lord will come again' (in the future), but what we should really be saying is 'The Lord is coming, coming, coming' (in the present).

'I am he who is, and was, and is to come...' (Rev.1.8). The Lord is the one who does not cease to come, because he is here. The Lord is here, we sing in the French mass, in a marvellous hymn which follows the consecration:

Christ has come.
Christ was born.
Christ has suffered.
Christ died.
Christ is risen.
Christ is alive.
Christ will come again.
Christ is here.

Yes, indeed he is here with us. Between his first and second coming, between the 'has appeared' and 'will come again', both of them visible and tangible, between this past and this future, there is the daily and continual coming of Christ in each one of us; there is the actuality of his active and hidden presence in history to bring this history to its consummation.

Another fine hymn which we know and love in the mass runs,

You are here at the heart of our lives
You make us live.

Here we have the presence of eternity at the heart of time, through Jesus Christ who gives meaning to time and history and who completely fulfils and renews them because God cannot enter into human history without turning everything upside down, without renewing and transforming everything. With this mystery which has been accomplished once and for all in Jesus Christ, at a stroke history has reached the level of eternity, anticipating its final destiny in what has been called the fullness of time. That's a very fine expression!

The fullness of time, which is the coming of Christ, does not simply mean that something precise happened at H-hour and D-Day. The expression 'fullness of time' means more than that. It means that in Jesus Christ there is a summing up, a recapitulation of fullness:

For in him all the fullness of God was pleased to dwell...

For in him the whole fullness of deity dwells bodily (Colossians 1.19; 2.9).

In the historical event of Jesus, time in some way contracts, concentrates itself, adds itself up. Jesus Christ embraces all history within himself and sums it up. In other words, this history which unrolled itself before him and which will prolong itself after him is wholly present in him, and that is why he has been able to redeem it.

To say that Jesus is the Alpha and Omega presupposes that the thirty-three years which he lived are in fact, in a mystery which is beyond our comprehension, the total history of humankind, time concentrated in its totality. If this were not the case, Christ would not be the Alpha and the Omega; he would be simply a man who was born in the year 4 BC in the reign of the Emperor Augustus and who died in the year 29 under the Emperor Tiberius and when Pontius Pilate was governor of Judaea: a historical, temporal and finite being – like you or me.

The reality of Christ infinitely surpasses the narrow limits of historical life. Men like John and Paul were able to recognize in this being of flesh and blood called Jesus of Nazareth the head of humanity, the one who embraces history in his person and then transcends it. Now the mystery of Jesus, the Alpha and Omega, the First and the Last, the living one, illuminates our mystery and makes sense of our lives. How does it do that? To answer this question we must first reflect on the significance of time.

Time is the place of the creature, the place of becoming; it expresses the distance between 'us' and 'us'; it is a space in which we fulfil ourselves. We are in time because we are created. And because we are created, we begin and we end. But we begin in the form of a seed and we end in the form of a tree which has realized all the potentialities contained in the seed. Between our beginning and our end, between our birth and our death, there is a development and a growth by which we become what we are; we realize that we were only potential. Time allows this transition from the potential to the actual. That is why time is creative.

The time in which my existence unfolds is not just a duration in which I can simply live, subsist; it is a time which realizes and constructs something. The time of the living being, the time of the human being, is a time which creates, which arouses, which brings about development. One might ask why God, rather than making us seeds, did not make us trees all at once, in other words why he did not make us beings who from the start had completely realized themselves. That would have saved us all kinds of troubles and difficulties. Why did he impose on us this puzzling and laborious process of making our own selves? Why go this long way round, with all these complications? Why not create us at point Z instead of at point A?

The reason is that if God had created us at point Z, we would no longer be human beings, but completely finished things, stable, immobile, immutable. By contrast, human beings are those who, as Sartre put it, make themselves, create themselves, decide themselves, choose themselves.

Human beings choose themselves, and time is the sphere in which they have the possibility of making this choice. In this sense we call time creative, since it is to time that human beings owe the possibility of becoming and shaping themselves.

In God, the distance between 'us' and 'us' does not exist, since God *is*; God does not *become*. That is why we say that God is eternal. If God were subject to a process of becoming, he would be temporal, he would be a creature as we are, he would be caught up in a duration as we are. Hegel wanted to introduce the notion of becoming into God, making history the sphere in which God realizes himself. For Hegel, the absolute Spirit realizes itself only in the succession that we call history. That is unacceptable. God is God from all eternity. He is the Alpha and Omega from all eternity. God does not undergo any development.

However, by creating a world, this God who is himself from all eternity involved himself in it so as to allow it to come into being, and that is what explains the transition from the less to the more which we call development and evolution.

How is it that in the creaturely world we can observe such a movement from the lesser to the greater? How can it be that the lesser gives rise to a greater? How can a small, hard and bitter seed grow into a tree full of sweet fruits? How can a tiny embryo result in a tall, intelligent human being?

According to the strict laws of logic, mathematics and physics, it would seem impossible for the greater to emerge from the lesser. That is inconceivable. But in evolution we are confronted with this riddle: starting from atoms and pure matter, we have life, plants, animals and finally human beings. This development, this progress, this ascending movement is strictly inexplicable, since the lesser cannot produce the greater. However, it is in fact evident every day that the tree shoots up, human beings grow and mature, the world evolves. How can that be?

The answer is that it is possible because eternity is at the heart of time.

Let us reflect on creation and becoming.

Classical philosophy has accustomed us to consider the world

42]

as a static entity, the existence of which is self-sustaining down through history. This conception gave rise to two terms in scholastic theology: 'creation' and the 'sustaining of being'. The world was once created by God and since then God has kept it in being as it is. God cares for its preservation, its existence.

The disadvantage of such a view of the world is that it overlooks the fact that creative being at the same time underlies the becoming, the development of the world. It is not the case that the world is; rather, it is coming to be.

It is to the great credit of contemporary science that it has struggled so hard with this coming to be. The world was not created in its present state, as our ancestors believed, but is the result of a long upward process which not only involves the sheer transformation and metamorphosis of being, but also clearly displays a real progress.

Between the atom and the cell, as between the cell and *homo sapiens*, we can observe not only an alteration and an interesting transformation of being, but above all a change from the lesser to the greater. This change is not a quantitative but a qualitative progress.

But why should a qualitative progress call for a lesser cause than a quantitative process? Why do people expect a greater creative power for the creation of a piece of matter from nothing (*ex nihilo*) than for the creation of life from matter (*ex materia*) or for the appearance of the spirit from the living flesh (*ex vivo*)?

My view is that the immense distance between nothingness and primal matter is relatively small, compared with the infinite distance between matter and spirit. I believe that the fact of a qualitative growth applies equally to both the idea of creation and the 'production of matter' from nothing. The great Islamic theologian Ali al-Ashari, who died in Baghdad in 935, was right in suggesting that anyone who wants to prove the existence of a creator God need only contemplate the qualitative growth of life.

The one thing which makes us hesitate to say that the way from the lower to the higher, from the lesser to the greater, is as inexplicable as that from nothingness to being, is purely and simply the frequency with which we encounter it. In our environment, and in our own persons, we are so accustomed to this 'process of nature' that we regard it as normal. But if we attempted to renew our capacity for wonder, then we could become philosophers and sages. And then we would soon concede that in the whole of 'natural evolution' there is a qualitative increase from the lesser to the greater, and an explanation has to be found for this. Anyone who puts a bet on 'nature' will win nothing; that does not explain the problem but simply shifts it elsewhere.

Do we not find the only satisfactory answer if we say that all events have one and the same cause? The primal matter produced at the origin of cosmic existence contained the substratum for the whole of evolution, but at the same time also that inner quality of many-sided growth which was to lead it to its goal. From beginning to end of this development the cause is one and the same, both in its quantitative extension and in its inner development and maturing.

So the goal of created being is not just its preservation and increase in a quantitative sense – such a view of things would be too simple for this grandiose enterprise of creation; it would not be enough. God not only sustains a being which he has created but allows it to become. And this becoming is both creation and preservation; the two things are identical.

Creation takes place every day before our eyes; we experience it every day, and it is far from having come to an end. Creation, evolution, incarnation, history and eschatology are essentially one and the same event. All follow one and the same movement, and above all, have one and the same cause. This one cause is God, who at the origin of the world produced a crude, formless and inwardly empty matter from nothing and made it fertile with his spirit, so that it could slowly be encouraged to rise upwards and after a twofold metamorphosis achieve its crowning glory – in the kingdom of God.

Time and history have a higher principle than themselves which makes possible this rising development from the lesser to the greater. It is really inconceivable that I should develop and grow as much as I do both physically and in other respects if there is no more in me than myself. If there were no more in me than myself I would always be the same, in a state of perpetual stagnation. But since there is growth and development, then there is within me a principle of growth and development, an element within me which is more than me and which acts as a catalyst, a motive power that drives me forward and upward.

God's eternity at the heart of time is the condition which allows time to be creative, and allows the world to grow and evolve. In fact, time exists only in relation to other things than itself. It is because the eternal is within time that time takes on a value. So, far from devaluing time, eternity gives it value – provided that eternity is understood as a mystery within time.

But if time is separated from the eternal which gives it life from within, the movement is reversed, and time, far from being creative, becomes destructive. Time is not automatically creative. Time is creative only when it is indwelt by eternity and animated by it. If it is separated and detached, it becomes a time of regression and death or a time of sin.

We do not have to believe that eternity is at the heart of time like a destiny which forces time to progress and rise higher. That may perhaps be true until the appearance of human beings, but with human beings a new element appears, that of a choice for or against this inner thrust, for or against this growth and self-conquest, a movement towards being more.

The time of choice is the time of acceptance or rejection, and if there is rejection, there is regression, a fall backwards towards death, which is what we call sin. In the time of sin there is no longer creation, but de-creation, to use a term of Simone Weil's. There is dispersion, decomposition.

By contrast, the time of grace is the time when human beings open themselves to eternity, which lures them from within and allows them to be borne up by it. Those who do this arrive at another dimension of being, beyond themselves, and participate in the very eternity of God. As Péguy put it:

And eternity itself is in the temporal,
And the tree of the race is deeply rooted,
goes deep into the soil and reaches right to its foundation,
and time itself is a timeless time.

This fusing of time and eternity came about historically in the incarnation, thanks to which the living spring of God has become our spring! By opening ourselves to it, we share in God's life and in this spring. In two texts from St John, the story of the woman of Samaria (4.10) and the story of the Feast of Tabernacles (7.37-39), Jesus expresses this profound truth: 'He who believes in me, out of his heart shall flow rivers of living water... The water that I shall give him will become in him a spring of water welling up to eternal life.'

The faith which is this acceptance of God as the spring at the heart of my life means that in turn I become what God is – a spring. This is the unheard-of mystery of faith and hope at which we arrive thanks to the reality of the incarnation.

God is at the heart of history.
God is at the heart of time.
God is in the human heart.

God is there as an explosive force which gives our life a new dimension and our existence an infinite value. From now on each of our moments is full of his presence, since eternity is at the heart of time. The irruption of eternity into time confers upon time a fullness of being, a weight of reality and being, a density of meaning which it is incapable of having by itself. From now on nothing in our lives is insignificant or ordinary; the most trivial act can be transfigured by this truth of faith.

We have tended to divide our actions into achievements and ordinary activities. To be in charge of a school or a business is an achievement; to sweep a room or to cook are ordinary activities. Starting from this conception we have established a hierarchy without taking account of the fact that what gives value to an action is not the action itself but the spirit in which it is done. Nothing is trivial, nothing is ordinary for someone whose life draws on the eternal.

I can still hear upset nuns complaining at having been assigned to cooking or to kindergarten when they could have been superiors or taught in secondary schools. They felt diminished, misunderstood, humiliated. What nonsense! Did the Virgin Mary do anything other than cook, go to the market and sweep the house? She did not have any glorious achievements, did not perform any miracles! And yet she represents the supreme figure of human history.

The gospel constantly reveals to us that what is lowest is in fact highest, that the last shall be first and the first last. If we understood that and really accepted it, how many of our complexes would disappear! The essential thing is not what I do but the significance that I attach to what I do. Once that happens, nothing is ordinary any more, and the most trivial reality is transfigured and takes on a divine and eternal dimension.

Another idea emerges from this involvement of the eternal in the temporal: each of our moments is unique. Time is irreversible; it passes and never passes by again. It escapes us, and it is no use running after it to try to catch it, like someone running after a shadow at sunset. There's no point in running after your shadow: you'll never catch it up. It's also the same for those who run after time. There is no point in being foolish or panicking. The irreversibility of time is not a catastrophe; on the contrary, it is something which gives importance to each of my choices. What gives the action that I do here and now its eternal value is what gives my existence its value and its weight.

In the previous chapter I quoted the beautiful verse by Countess de Noailles, 'We shall never be able to call our souls our own more than we can this evening.' I did not want simply to express a vague and more or less sentimental nostalgia, but to convey that each of our moments is unique. Now is a serious moment, since it is the place where I am going to perform an action which involves all my being, and consequently takes on the value of eternity. So for us the irreversibility of time is the occasion for taking the passing moment seriously.

In his fine book *Existence and Eternity*, Fernand Guimet remarked:

The irreversibility of time, in the Christian perspective of existence, has a different meaning from this succession of hours, all of which hurt us and the last of which kills us. It allows us to measure the seriousness of an existence which is given us only once, an existence in which every day and every hour counts, and in which every day and every hour does not cease to be the day and the hour when we respond to our eternal vocation.

This is a very powerful idea, because it provokes us. When I think that I am in my fifties, I ask myself: 'Lord, what have I done with the past fifty years of my life? And what will I do with the years to come, in which each month, each day, each hour, each minute, bring a unique message?' Each passing moment I have to do something full, something overflowing. If time is irreversible, it is no use complaining and telling myself, 'It's terrible, time's passing'. I have to seize it with both hands and involve all my being in it so as not to waste the slightest bit of it.

What makes me mad here in Egypt is the total absence of a sense of the value of time amongst the majority of people. What value can it have for men aged thirty, forty or fifty, spending hours every morning playing tric-trac or smoking water pipes in cafés?

Does time have any value for them? Between June and October several million young Egyptians ask themselves what they are going to do with their holidays. They spend four months on a mat on the beach and at discos in the evening, to kill time. Four months wasted – completely lost – in the full flush of youth. Can you imagine it?

Time is a treasure to be exploited, capital to bring profit, a talent to develop. What do we do with it? What have we done with it? For us the irreversibility of time is a challenge to accept, a challenge to provoke us. In the last century the French poet Lamartine dreamed of stopping time as Joshua is said one day to have stopped the sun. But you don't stop time by stopping the sun; you stop time by plunging into it and surpassing it. For the sun to stop doesn't change anything – it is men and women who have to stop and learn how to penetrate the heart of time in order to find eternity in it.

This brings us to the way in which we experience time: it can be both cyclical and linear. Cyclical time is a movement of indefinite repetitions in which nothing new happens. This idea is expressed very well at the beginning of the biblical book of Ecclesiastes:

Vanity of vanities! All is vanity.
What does a man gain by the toil
at which he toils under the sun?
A generation goes, and a generation comes,
but the earth remains for ever.
The sun rises, and the sun goes down,
and hastens to the place where it rises.
The wind blows to the south, and goes round to the north,
round and round goes the wind,
and on its circuits the wind returns.
All streams run to the sea, but the sea is not full;
to the place where the streams flow, there they flow again.
All things are full of weariness, a man cannot utter it;
the eye is not satisfied with seeing, nor the ear filled with
     hearing.
What has been is what will be,
and what has been done is what will be done,
and there is nothing new under the sun.
Is there a thing of which it is said,

'See, this is new'?
It has been already,
in the ages before us.

The Hebrew Koheleth, author of this biblical text, is quite pessimistic: 'Nothing new under the sun.'

'Nothing new under the sun...' That reminds me of a surprising conversation which I had one day up at the top of the Great Pyramid with a guide with whom I had climbed up. He assured me that the ancient Egyptians had already discovered all the inventions of our age five thousand years ago: rifles, rockets, planes, the atom bomb and the rest of it. And he added, 'We have not discovered anything which did not exist before. We have simply lost trace of it.'

Nor is he the only one. Many pseudo-scientific books and journals claim the same thing and enjoy wide circulations. We are told that everything had already been discovered in the past, but that this brilliant civilization was swallowed up by a terrible cataclysm. Humanity then began to develop all over again, and nowadays we are simply rediscovering what our ancestors had already discovered in times past. But what is equally old is this cyclical concept of time. Here is a text from antiquity: the author is Nemesius, who lived around AD 400.

Socrates, Plato and each individual will live again with the same friends and companions. They will have the same experiences and the same activities. Every city, every village, every field will be restored to its former state. This restoration of the universe will not be done once for all, but will have to be done again and again, ceaselessly, for all eternity. The gods, who are not subject to destruction, having observed the course of events in a period, will know what must happen in all subsequent periods. For there will be nothing new – and nothing will happen which has not always existed down to the smallest detail.

Here we can find the same tone that we heard in the Hebrew Koheleth, the preacher of Ecclesiastes, and in modern times Nietzsche says precisely the same thing.

'O Zarathustra,' said the animals then, 'all things themselves dance for such as think as we: they come and offer their hand and laugh and flee – and return.
  Everything goes, everything returns; the wheel of existence

[49

rolls for ever. Everything dies, everything blossoms anew; the year of existence runs on for ever.

Everything breaks, everything is joined anew; the same house of existence builds itself for ever. Everything departs, everything meets again; the ring of existence is true to itself for ever' (*Thus Spake Zarathustra*, 'The Convalescent').

So your life has already been lived hundreds, thousands, millions of times, and you are simply beginning your existence all over again. In a book called *The Myth of the Eternal Return* the famous ethnologist Mircea Eliade has given a magisterial account of this cyclical concept of time as history eternally beginning all over again.

In any case, does not astrology suppose that our destiny is predetermined? The stars, which have been witnesses to what happened on earth in former times and in our former lives, can reveal our future to us. So there are people who avidly scrutinize their morning paper to know what kind of a day they will be having. As if my day was already pre-programmed, was no more than a predetermined destiny to which I have to submit!

But that is not the case. My morning paper does not tell me what kind of a day I'm going to have. My day will be what I make it. 'What's going to happen to me today?' That's something that I shall be deciding, and this morning will be mine: it will not belong to Mars, Neptune or Jupiter. I am utterly opposed to the astral fatalism which is emerging again in our day; it is simply an expression of our avoidance of responsibility and our fear of freedom, the fear of personal commitment.

This cyclical concept of time as an eternal return of phenomena has deep roots in the countryside and in rural society. For all their lives peasants experience this repetitive cycle of nature. The sun rises and the sun sets; the Nile rises in August and falls in October; night follows day and day follows night; the same rhythm of the seasons is repeated every year: spring, summer, autumn, winter. Birth yields to death and death yields to birth. All this gives country people the feeling of eternally new beginnings in which nothing really new ever happens.

By contrast, city people, those who live in industrial societies, have escaped the fatality of a cyclical time and discovered the linear dimension of time. With the coming of the modern age, time takes on a direction, is aimed towards an end, develops towards a goal, tends towards a realization. Time becomes a history.

For example, try to imagine the revolution that the Aswan Dam has brought about for the Egyptian peasants, who for millennia had become accustomed to the inundation from the Nile every summer and had regulated their lives by it. Suddenly, by the decision of a man called Nasser, the Nile has stopped rising every year, and as a consequence the whole countryside is electrified, completely upsetting the very cycle of day and night. All this represents an enormous revolution in the mind of the Egyptian peasants within a few years, utterly overturning their view of the world.

Human beings suddenly discover that they themselves make history, that they themselves decide on their lives, that they themselves can make day or night by switching on the electric light, that the Nile can rise or fall at their command, that it will rain or not rain, depending on the techniques that are applied. It is no longer the case that human beings are subject to time, but rather that time is subject to human beings. Human beings escape the fatalism of the cycle and become masters of history.

In such a conception, God no longer finds his place in history as the one who governs nature, since from now on human beings have taken his place. So it is no coincidence that atheism has appeared along with the birth of the modern age and the industrial era. Here human beings escape the fatalism of a 'natural' time and create their own time, a 'human' time, that of work, of machines, factories, choice, freedom. And at the same time they discover that time has a value: time is money. Unfortunately those who frequent the cafés of Egypt have not yet made this discovery; they are still living in the other time, the old time, when nothing happened. Time is not money for them!

I have made a distinction between cyclical time and linear time. In fact, neither expresses the objective reality of time. Time is neither cyclical nor linear, but spiral; that is to say, we simultaneously begin again and go forward. We do not just begin again by returning to the starting point, but as we go round in circles, we gradually rise to a higher stage of development. The sun which rises today is indeed the same sun that rose yesterday and will rise tomorrow, but everything happens within time: the earth is different, human beings have changed, history has developed. And yet there is repetition – however, it is a repetition which brings about progress, which produces a plan, which tends towards an eschatology.

This idea of eschatology seems to have originated in Judaism and Christianity, because it is said in the Bible that history has a beginning and an end; it is enclosed within an Alpha and an Omega. Ontology becomes an eschatology. The Christian conception of time is an evolutionary conception in which time is creative, history has a goal and temporality acquires a meaning. In this perspective, the incarnation is a unique event which cannot be repeated; the cross is a unique event which cannot be repeated; the life of Christ is an event which cannot be repeated; and human life is also a unique event which cannot be repeated.

In this context, I would like to quote a passage from the Letter to the Hebrews which may shed light on what I have just said:

> Nor was it to offer himself repeatedly, as the high priest enters the Holy Place yearly with blood not his own; for then he would have had to suffer repeatedly since the foundation of the world. But as it is, he has appeared once for all at the end of the age to put away sin by the sacrifice of himself. And just as it is appointed for men to die once, and after that comes judgment, so Christ, having been offered once to bear the sins of many, will appear a second time, not to deal with sin but to save those who are eagerly waiting for him (9.25-28).

This idea of unrepeatable time demonstrates the unique character of the phenomenon of the incarnation and the unique character of our own existence. So the idea of eschatology frees us from the fleeting nature of time and the nightmare of entropy. According to the law of entropy, the world is constantly involved in an irreversible and irreparable loss of energy. Electric lights consume energy which is lost for ever. Every day the sun burns up energy which is lost for ever and cannot be renewed. The world is therefore orientated on a progressive loss of energy which means that we are all threatened, sooner or later, with the prospect of the eternal cold. Science tells us that the world is growing old, is using itself up, is impoverishing itself irreparably, and that one day this process will result in the total death of the universe. Such a view, which is true, real and scientific, cannot but engender in us pessimism, despair and darkness.

However, at this point faith comes in, announces itself, and demands a hearing. Faith tell us that such a dying of the world and human beings is a transition to another sphere or state, and that something is already going on behind a 'curtain'; something new is in preparation. The believer 'knows' that, so we talk of our knowledge of faith, that goes a long way, even extending to eschatology.

To explain all this more closely, Teilhard de Chardin describes the working of two kinds of energy: tangential or material energy, like the sun or an electric light bulb, and radial or spiritual energy. Tangential or material energy is subject to constant loss because it is subject to the phenomenon of entropy; by contrast, radial or spiritual energy does not cease growing and increasing in inverse proportion to material energy. So there is a rise in the spiritual and psychical in our world, an exchange between these two forms of energy, in favour of love, in favour of a rise of consciousness and a development of consciousness. So we are told by Teilhard de Chardin, who behind the apparent decline of our world recognized and experienced its true rise – its radial growth. Eternity at work in history is in process of giving birth to a new world, an eternal morning. And that is just what Easter means. Easter is a morning which does not pass away, an eternal morning.

The resurrection of Christ is a triumph over death and the basis of human history, making it flow into the eternal and the definitive. In Christ, the passage of all humankind to the other shore, to life eternal, to triumph over death, is accomplished once for all, since Christ is the Alpha and the Omega, who sums up all human history in himself.

Because Christ is man, Son of Man, perfect man, total man, what happens in him has already happened in each one of us. When St Paul claims that 'You are risen with Christ and your life is hidden in God' (Col.3.13), he is making a very profound statement. Christian hope is based on the conviction that the definitive act of salvation in human history has already been performed, already achieved, already accomplished in Christ. It is based on the conviction that in him we escape death and night, that beyond this transitory world there is another world inside this world which does not pass away, crossing it and transcending it. So the eternity which breaks into time with Jesus Christ and which has culminated in the resurrection gives the present all its density.

Here is another quotation from Fernand Guimet:

Our present is now no longer this ridge walk along a knife edge which we are constantly invited to cross, between the slope of a past which is no longer and that of a future which is yet to be.

Beyond the very order of fugitive time, in a kind of *stasis* which is as it were a potential *ekstasis*, ecstasy, it is rather, or at least, called to be the phenomenology of the presence of God and his grace. In faithfulness to the Spirit, it is the place of our encounter with God, the place of a conversion in which everything is always open to us, by the very grace of the Easter mystery, the place of a passage from this world to the Father.

Eschatology has already become present in history. The definitive triumph of humanity in Christ is already achieved and present. That is why Christ can say that 'The kingdom of God is within you... The kingdom of God is among you... The kingdom of God is here' (Matt.12.28; Luke 17.21).

Christ knew that he bore human history within himself; he knew that his coming was the definitive coming of God on earth; he knew that his resurrection was also the resurrection of the world.

Finally, here is one last idea. The presence of eternity at the heart of time, by the incarnation and the resurrection of Christ, is a principle of continuous development and renewal in human beings and in history. The irruption of God at the heart of the world evokes the unexpected, the inexplicable, the unforeseen, which escape all scientific forecasts, including those of that modern science which calls itself futurology.

In the world there is always more than the world; in history there is always more than history; in human beings there is always more than their human nature.

Who could have foreseen John XXIII or the Second Vatican Council in the second half of our century? That was an utterly unexpected event, and one which changed the course of history. Who could have foreseen Einstein, whose theories overturned modern science? Who could have foreseen the developments in our time which have utterly confounded all our predictions? What will the next discovery be? What will the human race look like in twenty years time?

We are told of all kinds of disasters and upheavals which will take place in the year 2000. What will we know about them? Some people tell us that the world is so evil that the end must be very near. Others say that our human race is so old that its end is imminent. But God works wonders with the elderly! He raises up men and women, prophets, saints, geniuses, new ideas, new inventions, at the most unexpected moments and among the most critical periods.

Christ told us, 'Do not be anxious for the morrow' (Matt.6.34), and when he said this he meant both individuals and humankind. Certainly, we need to be warned about the future, but within reason. Above all we must have trust. The one who has borne up the history of the universe for twenty billion years will bring this history to its conclusion. The past is the guarantee of the future. The Lord already tells us in the gospel, 'Be of good cheer, I have overcome the world' (John 16.33). I have already won the battle. I have already gained the triumph.

If Christians have an optimistic view of history, it is not as a result of simplistic bliss or passive expectation, but in the name of this certainty of faith that the divine has broken into the world in Jesus Christ and that this new element brings with it an immense hope. From now on, history surpasses itself, thanks to this divine ferment.

> The kingdom of heaven is like leaven which a woman took and hid in three measures of flour until it was all leavened (Matt.13.33).

> The kingdom of God is like a grain of mustard seed which is the smallest of all seeds but which becomes a great tree (Matt.13.31f.).

This seed hidden in the earth on the evening of Good Friday is in process of growing until the fullness of the kingdom which is to come. 'When I am raised up from the earth I will draw all people to me' (John 12.32).

Something enormous is going on within our history. The Lord has come. The Lord will come again. The Lord is coming. That is our hope.

I recently held a retreat in Alexandria during Lent on the theme of 'Human Hope and Christian Confidence'. I tried to explain that human hope is a short-term feeling which counts on known realities that often get out of hand. No wonder, then, that we are all dismayed at what goes on around us. By contrast, Christian confidence is focussed on realities which do not yet exist, which are in process of coming to be and are not yet manifest. It is an act of faith in the future, a bet on the one who made the world, who sowed the stars, the suns and the galaxies in space, and who is quite capable of raising up children of Abraham from these stones.

God makes fun of our prognostications, our predictions and our forecasts, since the one who creates heaven and earth does not cease to make us grow every day. 'My Father is working still, and I am working' (John 5.17). Christian faith is an enormous matter, a principle of hope and dynamism capable of overturning everything and moving mountains.

I believe in humankind because I believe in Jesus Christ.

I believe in the future because I believe in Jesus Christ.

What this future will be I do not know. Do not try to make plans for the future city. Do not try to describe the kingdom of God which is to come. The Apocalypse, which seeks to do this, necessarily remains vague and full of symbolism. We must not try to over-interpret these symbols; it is good that they remain vague.

The future is unpredictable, and even Karl Marx, who spoke of the future city, refused to describe it. For who could describe what the world and humankind will be like at the end of their evolution? Who could conceive of this kingdom which awaits us at the end of history?

Eye has not seen, nor ear heard, nor spirit imagined what God has prepared for those who love him (I Cor.2.9).

History is constantly new because the Spirit which is at work in history is constantly new. This Spirit constantly at work in the world is grace, the 'supplement of the soul' constantly breathed by God into the world. To live within the movement of the Spirit is to live in a state of grace, in this spirit of youth and childhood, which is to share in the eternal childlikeness of God. The child is someone who believes everything, hopes everything, dreams of the impossible; the child is someone who lives in a fairy-tale world, a utopian world, in the belief that it is all true – and children are right:

Truly, truly, I say you that unless you become like little children again, you will not enter the kingdom of God (Matt.18.3).

4 The Wisdom of Time

'Combine action with inaction and you won't go crazy'
(*Russian proverb*)

I want to begin with Saint-Exupéry's story of the little prince. The little prince had left his little planet, somewhere in the sky, and went to visit some other planets across the universe. The first of them was inhabited by an ambitious king and the second by a conceited man. The little prince had just been to the third planet, which was inhabited by a gloomy drunkard. The drunkard drank, he said, to forget that he was ashamed of himself. On each visit the little prince said, 'The grown-ups are certainly very, very odd'; on his travels he came to the fourth planet:

The fourth planet belonged to a businessman. This man was so much occupied that he did not even raise his head at the little prince's arrival.

'Good morning,' the little prince said to him. 'Your cigarette has gone out.'

'Three and two make five. Five and seven make twelve. Twelve and three make fifteen. Good morning. Fifteen and seven make twenty-two. Twenty-two and six make twenty-eight. I haven't time to light it again. Twenty six and five make thirty-one. Phew! So that makes five hundred and one million six hundred and eighty thousand seven hundred and thirty one.'

'Five hundred million what?' asked the little prince.

'Eh? Are you still there? Five hundred and one million – I can't stop... I've so much to do! I am concerned with matters of consequence. I don't amuse myself with balderdash. Two and five make seven...'

'Five hundred and one million what?' repeated the little

prince, who never in his life had let go of a question once he had asked it.

The businessman raised his head.

'During the fifty-four years I've inhabited this planet, I have been disturbed only three times. The first time was twenty-two years ago, when some giddy goose fell from goodness knows where. He made the most frightful noise that resounded all over the place, and I made four mistakes in my addition. The second time, eleven years ago, I was disturbed by an attack of rheumatism. I don't get enough exercise. I have no time for loafing. The third time – well, this is it. I was saying, then, five hundred and one millions...'

'Millions of what?'

The businessman realized that there was no hope of being left in peace until he answered this question.

'Millions of those little objects,' he said, 'which one some-times sees in the sky.'

'Flies?'

'Oh, no. Like glittering objects.'

'Bees?'

'Oh, no. Little golden objects that set lazy men to idle dreaming. As for me, I'm concerned with matters of conse-quence. There is no time for idle dreaming in my life.'

'Ah! You mean the stars?'

'Yes, that's it. The stars.'

'And what do you do with five hundred million stars?'

'Five hundred and one million, six hundred and twenty-two thousand seven hundred and thirty-one. I am concerned with matters of consequence; I am accurate.'

'And what do you do with these stars?'

'What do I do with them?'

'Yes.'

'Nothing. I own them.'

'You own the stars?'

'Yes.'

'But I have already seen a king who...'

'Kings do not *own*, they *reign* over. It is a very different matter.'

'And what good does it do you to own the stars?'

'It does the good of making me rich.'

'And what good does it do you to be rich?'

'It makes it possible for me to buy more stars, if any are discovered.'

And so on.

That's the story of the businessman. He counts the world, he counts the stars. He's busy, occupied, serious.

But the little prince isn't serious. He has time to spare, time to dream, time to look at the stars. The other man is serious. He counts, and counts again.

This story of the businessman reminds me of another story that you'll know.

> One day another businessman was going to work when he saw a bedouin from the desert sitting under a city palm tree resting and dreaming, as so many people do in Egypt. He stopped and said to him,
> 'What are you doing there?'
> The bedouin replied,
> 'As you can see, I'm dreaming, resting...'
> 'You know that you could be earning money if you were working.'
> 'What would I do with it?'
> 'If you earned money you could open an office.'
> 'And then?'
> 'Then you could earn more money and build a factory.'
> 'And then?'
> 'Then you could own a fine villa.'
> 'Good! And then?'
> 'Then you would still have money to put in the bank.'
> 'Yes. And then?'
> 'Then you could sit down and rest.'
> 'But that's what I'm doing at the moment.'

There are those among us who keep putting off the time when they can sit down and rest and in the end never get to the point of doing it: they never have time to sit down and rest because in fact they never finish their work. Just think about that a moment. When can you say that you've finished your work? Work never ends, whether you're a manager, a teacher, a worker, a director, a monk or a nun. There's always more to do, there's always work around, and you never finish it. If you wait until you've finished your work before you begin to live, you will never live. Take time to live! That's a wise thing to do. Hence the title of this chapter, 'The Wisdom of Time'.

This businessman is certainly intelligent, cultivated, serious, but perhaps he has not learned something that the bedouin at the foot of his tree has understood. He has not understood that time is something that one takes: otherwise it takes us; otherwise it is something that possesses us. Take time to live!

And the Lord who gave the commandments gave a third commandment: 'Keep the Lord's Day holy.' How do we do that? By going to mass? Not necessarily. Not primarily. There is no mass in the Old Testament. Then by doing what? By resting. Stop working. Not just you, but your manservant and your maidservant, your donkey and your ox. Give them time, time to live themselves.

So there is wisdom in this rest on the seventh day. The fact that the Lord gave a commandment about it should make us think. A divine commandment, one of God's ten commandments, is devoted to it, given over to the art of resting. So perhaps we shall see that there is a very close link between resting and praying. Rest itself is already prayer, and it is often because we have not rested that we do not know how to pray.

I spoke just now of finding time to live. And that is something which we people of the twentieth century, busy and overburdened, need to do.

Now I would like to talk about finding time to love. Let's go back to the little prince:

The fox gazed at the little prince, for a long time.

'Please – tame me,' he said.

'I want to, very much,' the little prince replied. 'But I have not much time. I have friends to discover and a great many things to understand.'

'One only understands the things that one tames,' said the fox. 'Men have no more time to understand anything. They buy things all ready made at the shops. But there is no shop anywhere where one can buy friendship, and so men have no friends any more. If you want a friend, tame me!'

'What must I do to tame you?,' the little prince asked.

'You must be very patient,' replied the fox. 'First you will sit down at a little distance from me – like that – in the grass. I shall look at you out of the corner of my eye, and you will say nothing. Words are the source of misunderstanding. But you will sit a little closer to me every day.'

Time to love. Friendship takes time. Love takes time. And often love dies for want of time and friendship dies for want of time. If we want to build up life together, and we do not give it the time it needs, that life will wither and die.

There used to be family meals at least once a day. A white tablecloth, flowers, napkins, glass. You went in before the meal, chatted, laughed, sat down. And then after the meal there was time to smile, to chat, to stay together. Now we have snack bars, fast food, self-service. Between-times you grab a sandwich, drink a Coke, on the go. You get home in the evening and either you aren't hungry because you've eaten too much or you eat straightaway without waiting for the others. Then you start work or go to bed. The others get in and do the same thing. People all eat when they want to, get up when they want to, have breakfast when they want to, go to bed when they want to.

The family meal is dead. You're lucky if there's time to have a meal together once a week. The proclamation of family life nowadays will not be found in great declarations; it is primarily and above all a way of being together, a way of living together.

Time is an indispensable element in forming a family; forming a family takes time. That is one of the demands of family life and at the same time one of its greatest joys. If you cannot count on giving time to your family, don't get married, because you will cheat your children and your spouse if you marry while knowing very well that you will have no time to give to them. To get married is to be prepared to give time to others: and that applies to giving time to husband or wife as well as to children. In fact, it is clear that if husband and wife themselves set an example in doing this, the children will join in: they will want to be there, they will enjoy being together, the family will attract them. And where there is a happy family life, the children develop well. Where there is no family life, the children have problems. Problem children are those with no real family life, who have seldom enjoyed a family meal, who have seldom experienced family reunions.

Time for loving also means outings together, walks, trips to the country or the shore, holidays abroad. That sort of thing brings the members of a family together. The fact of travelling together, of being elsewhere, in the midst of strangers in a strange world, immediately welds the family together. But that takes time.

If everything has to be expressed in terms of money, productivity, cash value, all this kind of time is lost time. But if we have another criterion of value in our time, if the ultimate value is not time and efficiency but joy and love – things which cannot be weighed or measured, which do not count – at that point we are capable of sacrificing. There would be loss on the one side but gain on the other, and this gain would be infinitely more precious that what we would have lost. There is always something to sacrifice; that's the price to be paid. Family life has its price, a couple's life together has its price, friendship has its price, love has its price – but one might say that it all pays off.

And the time we have to give cannot be condensed. We cannot concentrate compensation for hours or days of absence into a few short minutes' conversation. Any attempt to do that will seem like a grudged gift. No real encounters can take place in hasty meetings: they cannot result in mutual understanding. We live in an age of miniaturization, when everything is condensed: *Reader's Digest*, telex, multivitamins in a pill. I expect that one day we shall have the amazing opportunity, instead of taking three meals a day, wasting half an hour over each, to gulp down three pills which will save us this loss of time. Think of the satisfaction of working sixteen hours a day, of saving these three half-hours, of losing only three seconds to gulp down the pills! And roast turkeys with stuffing, apple pies and the rest will no longer exist – they will have been replaced by pills!

I hope that that age never comes; I hope that there will always be old wooden tables with glasses and napkins and the smell from the kitchen and long family meals. Don't dream of a concentrated family life, to which we give the absolute minimum, simply to reassure ourselves, to appease our conscience, to tell ourselves that we are doing our duty. Love cannot be condensed. We all need to ask ourselves whether we are taking time to love, to be with others, to enjoy ourselves with others. That's important.

I say that firmly to the clergy and to religious, because here I'm well aware of what I'm talking about. In the religious life you've never finished working; there's always something to do. But relax! If you are given time for recreation, spend it being with others, with your companions; forget your newspapers and magazines, put all your work on one side. Unwind with other people, chat, laugh, listen. I know someone who as soon as he comes into the common room picks up a newspaper. You talk to him and he replies, 'Yes, no, ah, well...' I'd like to pick up the newspaper, throw it out of the window, and say, 'Let's get rid of that. You can read it some other time. There's a time for laughing and a time for reading. Now's the time for laughing; you can read later.'

We might ask ourselves whether many problems in the family or between couples do not arise because they don't take time to be together.

I've spoken of family life. Let's talk for a while about the life of married couples. Husbands and wives must find time to be by themselves, perhaps at home, perhaps in their room, perhaps in a restaurant, perhaps going for a walk. Many marital problems arise and develop because the couple never talk. Things mount up, become burdensome, and poison life because they've never been talked about. And when they *are* talked about, they come out like cannon fire. Of course, it's inevitable that there should be such exchanges, but the cannons should then be given time to cool down. Perhaps the conversation will begin with complaints and home truths. Then, 'All right, what else do you have to say? and I'd like to tell you...' All this goes on, not just for quarter of an hour, but for two or three hours. Everything has to come out, the volcano has to erupt and calm down, the lava has to flow, so that the sun can shine again behind the volcano. Finally the couple can say, 'But in the end we can get over it all.'

We need time to listen: time to listen to our children, time to listen to one another. Parents need to take time to listen to their children when they've just come back from camp, from an excursion, from a trip. The children want to talk immediately, because they are full of their stories and their experience. They want to share what's happened, now! Never say to them, 'Not now, I'm busy. I'm tired.' When that happens, the days go by, the weeks go by and the child no longer wants to tell the story. There was just one occasion to hear it, and to deepen the relationship with your child, and you will have missed it.

Many problems with children arise precisely because there is no communication between parents and children. There's no time to listen. Listening is not easy and takes time. If you're in a hurry you won't listen. I'm incapable of talking to someone who keeps looking at his watch. To listen presupposes that one has time, all the time in the world, is perfectly relaxed, really present.

When someone asks me as a priest, 'Are you free?', I say, 'I'm always free.' One becomes free when that's important. I used to say: 'Free? How can I be free? I've a thousand things to do. I'm overburdened with work. You must be joking.' But it's important. I really am always free. In fact I'm always free and always busy. When it's important, I become free. The person in front of me must be given the impression that all my time is at his or her disposal. Some problems take ten minutes and don't need more. But these ten minutes are minutes given, minutes during which there is truly a reciprocal presence, communication. At that moment I've really given my ten minutes. There are other problems which take two or three hours. In fact, when you begin an interview you're never quite sure how long it's going to take.

I remember one of my friends telling me that there are problems for which the time-factor is indispensable if a solution is to appear. Psychologists are aware of that. Someone talks, and often says nothing. He or she talks and talks and talks. After an hour, an hour and a half, two hours, the real problem begins to emerge and there is a crisis: floods of tears. Often the problem is hidden and the person in front of me is unaware of it, or is afraid to mention it, is ashamed to speak of it – so the problem takes time to come out. And if you haven't taken the time, you will have sent the client away; he or she will have left with the problem and nothing will have been resolved. It's hard to take time to listen; it's an ascetic discipline, and at the same time it's an area in which one can hope to work at depth.

In psychology there is what is called logotherapy, from the Greek *logos*, word, and *therapein*, to cure. All psychology is based on that. An analysis can take three, four or five years, with sessions lasting two to three hours. I sympathize with the analyst. I remember a cartoon with the patient stretched out on the couch and the psychoanalyst asleep in his chair. The client was talking away and the analyst was fast asleep. Analysis takes a long time. One of the diseases of our time is the absence of communication, the lack of communication between people, communication in depth. Logotherapy aims at helping people to express all that they were unable to say, all that is bottled up inside them.

I have spoken of time to live, time to love and time to listen. Now I would like to say something about time to grow and mature. People only grow in time, and one cannot economize over time in growth or education. We know that all education requires a certain amount of time. But many ambitious parents do not know that by forcing their children through school too early or by arranging for them to jump a year they are not giving something but taking it away. As a result these children may become more aggressive, since they are too young for their class, suffer as a result, feel more pushed than the others and inferior to them. It could be a valuable help to such children if a skilled and sympathetic teacher 'failed' them and made them repeat a year, for in that way the child could gain self-confidence. The French Jesuit sociologist Desquéyrat commented that the quickest learners are not always the best twenty or thirty years later. Artificially accelerated development never helps anyone.

There are working-class boys who have never had a chance to go to school or university. At fourteen or fifteen they are little men. They began working as apprentices at the age of ten or eleven, earned money very soon and had family responsibilities. At fifteen they talk like men of twenty-five or thirty, but they always lack something. These personalities which have been formed too quickly have never known childhood, or adolescence, or youth, or the slow growth at the end of which a human personality is formed. They have matured too quickly on an improvised basis. They have not had their share of life and love, play and joy. Children who have never played can be very lively, but not having known childhood will have robbed them of something: it's a serious matter not to have been a child.

Children have to take their time; adolescents have to take their time; and in a way education, which retards maturity through school and university, is a good thing. The maturity comes later. Among the people I've just been talking about, a boy is mature at eighteen. In our societies, with school and university, a boy begins to become mature at twenty-five. I'm not insulting anyone here; it's not an insult – quite the contrary. The time you take to grow up isn't time lost; don't try to be grown up earlier than you need be. Adulthood will come all in good time, and when it does it will be a fully developed maturity, fully achieved, which will have taken time to come about. Things are better that way.

When I felt I had a vocation, I made inquiries to see whether I should become a Jesuit. When they told me that the training took fourteen years, I thought to myself: 'My God! I've had enough of school. Another fourteen years? These Jesuits must be crazy!' And then I understood. I understood that the Society of Jesus sacrificed a certain immediate efficiency, a rapid return (for I wanted to give, I was anxious to produce, to work, to act), for something deeper but longer-term. So I accepted the delay, this slow and patient growing to maturity, this long period of austere study for something more profound. There is wisdom there, and nothing to be regretted.

What do Bedouins write on the walls of their tents? 'Patience is the key to joy', or 'Patience is sweet'. Here's the same sentiment in another passage from Kazantzakis's *Zorba the Greek*:

> I remembered one morning when I discovered a cocoon in the bark of a tree, just as the butterfly was making a hole in its case and preparing to come out. I waited a while, but it was too long appearing and I was impatient. I bent over it and breathed on it to warm it. I warmed it as quickly as I could and the miracle began to happen before my eyes, faster than life. The case opened, the butterfly started slowly crawling out and I shall never forget my horror when I saw how its wings were folded back and crumpled; the wretched butterfly tried with its whole-trembling body to unfold them. Bending over it, I tried to help it with my breath. In vain. It needed to be hatched out patiently and the unfolding of the wings should be a gradual process in the sun. Now it was too late. My breath had forced the butterfly to appear, all crumpled, before its time. It struggled and, a few seconds later, died in the palm of my hand.
>
> That little body is, I do believe, the greatest weight I have on my conscience. For I realize today that it is a mortal sin to violate the great laws of nature. We should not hurry, we should not be impatient, but we should confidently obey the eternal rhythm.
>
> I sat on a rock to absorb this New Year's thought. Ah, if only that little butterfly could always flutter before me to show me the way!

We, too, are sometimes too hasty with our children, want them to mature too quickly, become wise too quickly, reasonable too quickly, adult too quickly. A child is not an adult; it is not even a small adult; it is a child. It has a rhythm to respect. And you don't make your child an adult by talking; there are some things which only come with time.

Paul Claudel has a fine phrase, 'You don't open a bud with your fingers.' That's splendid. You have a rosebud and you say, 'I want a flower, an open rose.' You pull on the petals with all your might, and all you get is a sorry mess. It's the same thing with children. Children don't open up through advice, or orders, or talk, or lectures: children open up when the climate is ripe. A child is timid because the climate in which it lives does not help it to open up. You say to the child, 'But don't be timid, shy and silent. Smile, talk, relax!' The more you press the child, the more he or she will remain shut in. You don't make a child open up like that, any more than you do a flower. Like a flower, the child needs an atmosphere of warmth – human warmth and confidence, a fond smile, a kind look; those help the child to blossom. It's not so much a technique as a climate, a matter of taking time.

I learned more about that when I was regional superior of the Jesuits in Egypt. I wanted to change the Society of Jesus in Egypt far too quickly, immediately. I arrived with plans and projects, and I saw that people were not following my rhythm. So I asked myself whether I wasn't making a mistake. You can't make people go as you can make machines and automobiles and locomotives and such things go. Human beings have their rhythm, their character, their temperament. Taking account of all this is a matter of wisdom, and I think that there is a time factor in all government. Being in charge of people means taking the time factor into one's calculations.

'The best fruits are those which fall by themselves when they are ripe,' said Ricciotti. To discover that is to accept the law of growth, the time of growth.

Now I want to talk about creative time, since time creates. An artist who has not been pregnant with a work for many months, has not had it circulating in the blood and beating in the heart, may produce something, but it will not be a real masterpiece. Why? Because it has not matured in time. Perhaps this is the explanation why so much contemporary art is valueless, however much people discuss it and however much they pay for it.

You may know Pascal's remark, 'He wrote a big book because he did not have time to write a little one.'

That's also true. Pressure to publish may produce a book which gets bigger and bigger because it has not had time to mature; the material increases as an attempt at a solution. Nowadays authors make use of the most modern technology to get a book out in record time. But where is the time that it needs to mature?

I once saw the corrections which La Fontaine made to his classic fables – they were extraordinary. A simple little fable which seemed to have sprung straight from La Fontaine's pen was in fact the result of scrupulous correction and patient labour. This simplicity is the result of a very long effort, painful asceticism, and infinite patience.

We can go back over centuries and millennia and note that nothing changes with regard to the great significance of the time factor for growth and maturity. Here I'm thinking of the book by Isha Schwaller de Lubicz, *Her-Bak*, about Pharaonic Egypt, which contains a conversation between Her-Bak, an apprentice potter aged thirteen, and his master.

'What's a masterpiece?' asked Her-Bak. The old potter reflected and then said, 'A masterpiece is something that one creates with one's soul, that one has conceived with one's heart, that one has formed with one's body, from the skin to the entrails, that one has experienced, that one has carried around until its due time like a ripe fruit. It is brought to birth with the fingers.'

Her-Bak pondered.

'Does it take long to make a masterpiece?'

'Generations prepare for it. A man, their heir, produces it.'

'What do you have to do to be such a man?'

'Listen to the voice of the ancients, observe nature, and keep quiet.'

This is a very fine text. The old artist expresses what he sees: the work is deep within him, in the confused state of a feeling, an emotion, an intuition. What form will it take, what appearance will it assume? He does not yet know. The work has to mature slowly, with a long period of gestation. The artist is like the pregnant woman who feels that her time has come. And like the child, the work of art then emerges of its own accord.

The same thing can be said of poetry. The great Austrian poet Rainer Maria Rilke once said that to write a single verse one had to have seen many cities and known many people, have a good understanding of animals and plants, so good that one could feel what it was like for a bird to fly or for a flower to open up in the morning. A verse should be the plunder of a full life: all that one carries around with oneself concentrated in ten lines. If that happens, then the ten lines will be good.

Rilke might have been exaggerating a bit, deliberately, but at least he points out the need for a very thorough observation of the world and quiet meditation. You have to let the outside world come into your body to taste it, to let it enter your heart, to contemplate it there and nowhere else. Only then can this world be born a second time, shining like a star, in the words of poetry. A true poem is a marriage between the world and human beings, between nature and the human heart. Only from this marriage of love can the true poet create.

All creation has its roots in time. It is in time that we have the soul of all things. How does it happen that we rediscover ourselves in one or other work of an author? 'That's just what I would have wanted to say: it's a perfect expression of how I feel.' In fact, by reaching to the very depths, the writer meets the point at which we all converge, at which we all meet, the focal point of all human communication.

Now I want to talk about the time of knowing. Not learning, but knowing. Paul Claudel showed how the French for knowing, '*connaître*', can be read as '*con-naître*', being born with. To know someone is to be born with that person, to share a new beginning with him or her, for all knowledge immerses us in time.

Nature itself gives us abundant examples, for nature is a school. Look at the sun. It is dawn, it is mid-day, it is sunset. Hardly has the sun appeared above the horizon than it rises a little, slowly, slowly, imperceptibly, until it has gone right round the sky. The sun is never in a hurry; the moon and the stars are never in a hurry. Nature is never in a hurry. Everything revolves in this world, everything moves, and no one notices it.

Look at a tree. Between yesterday and today the tree has not changed, and yet it has changed. A plant has not changed, and yet it has changed. Something very profound is going on. Slowly the roots are penetrating the soil, slowly the branches are stretching towards the sky, but you can't see it; you never notice it. True growth is slow and imperceptible. True knowledge also immerses us in time.

Once, after giving a lecture in Alexandria on the Trinity, I was asked how long it had taken me to prepare. I replied, 'Thirty years' – and that was true. For the two or three hours' immediate preparation for the lecture were simply a gathering together of ten thousand elements gleaned from my whole life: thoughts, feelings, emotions, experiences long savoured and loved which I had only to put together as a bouquet, as a sheaf. You don't prepare for a lecture in an hour or a month, but all your life. Unless words emerge from the depth of one's soul, from the depth of one's being, they have no value, no savour. There is a whole difference between a truth learned and a truth lived.

Unfortunately, in most schools truths already learned are handed on, no more, and that is why they are so quickly dead as far as the pupils are concerned: accumulated knowledge, catalogued truths, an indigestible and inassimilable farrago which the pupils rapidly spew out and reject once the examination is over. That's a good thing, because if it remained in their stomachs it would kill the poor things. Any knowledge which has not entered into your flesh, your skin, your heart, remains external and alien to you. Reject it, because it will do you more harm than good. Learning 'by heart' is not a matter of accumulating knowledge in the reservoir of memory or dulling the mind with figures, dates and names; it is primarily learning 'with the heart', savouring, enjoying. Then such knowledge becomes an integral part of one; it becomes oneself.

That's the difference between culture and erudition. Culture is growth of the being by organic assimilation and the living integration of knowledge which is deeply loved and enjoyed. By contrast, erudition is a collection of miscellaneous and undigested baggage. The erudite person is a walking encyclopedia.

We should not be surprised that our young people do not enjoy going to school and are not keen to learn. There is nothing amazing about that, since school has become a vast collective enterprise engaged in dulling the mind, in intellectual sterilization and mental intoxication. The word for study in current Egyptian is *zakara*, i.e. to memorize: a formidable storing up of unformed and badly assimilated knowledge.

When I began my training as a Jesuit I discovered a new world. I left school sick and tired of all that I had learned. And suddenly I found an extraordinary delight in reading, getting to know, studying. A profound truth slowly began to take root deep with me, developing and growing; it helped me to mature and filled me with immense joy. I said to myself, 'How enjoyable learning is!' That's culture: a tree that grows, not a truck one fills; this new knowledge can be a sparkling spring.

Here are two quotations from the contemporary Swiss theologian Hans Urs von Balthasar:

Patience is the prime virtue of anyone who wants to learn. Only what has disappeared in the ear can be born in the heart.

And I would add:

Only what has been born in the heart can be repeated by the tongue.

Rudyard Kipling made the same point in his famous poem:

If you can trust yourself when all men doubt you,
but make allowance for their doubting too;
If you can dream – and not make dreams your master
If you can think – and not make thoughts your aim,
If you can meet with Triumph and Disaster
And treat those two impostors just the same...
you'll be a Man, my son!'

But who can take time to do all these things? Who can take time to dream, to think?

Saint-Exupéry said:

My people need time, if only to look at a tree. To sit down each day on the threshold in front of the same tree with the same branches. And little by little the tree reveals itself to them.

One day is not enough. It takes days and days until, little by little, the tree reveals its soul to us. It's the same with human beings. It takes time to get to know us, to discover us, because human beings do not reveal themselves all at once; they take time to uncover their souls. And that presupposes a look, a long look; waiting, long waiting; patience, long patience: until the other reveals himself or herself in a truth and a mystery which is very different from what we had originally imagined.

It's the same with God. It takes time to get to know God and discover God. And that presupposes that one takes time to pray. God does not reveal himself to anyone who is in a hurry. To penetrate his mystery, you have to take time, all your time.

Remember Jacob's ladder. Jacob went to sleep and in a dream he saw a long ladder reaching up to heaven with angels going up and down it. He woke up and exclaimed, 'God was there and I did not know it' (Gen.28.16). Jacob had to stop, rest, go to sleep, dream, before he suddenly realized that God was there.

It's the same with us. We have the impression that God is the great absentee figure. 'Lord, where are you? Reveal yourself!' We want God to reveal himself to us, like the light which comes on when we press the switch. We live in a mechanized world in which everything obeys our commands: the century of technology, the century of electronics, the century of switches and buttons. We want rapid, effective, automatic reactions. 'Lord, what do you have to tell me? Tell me quickly, in three words.' It's like someone saying to a beloved, 'Come on, quickly, do you love me or don't you?' People want meditation pills in three minutes, mini-meditations. Since everything is condensed in the modern world, why doesn't the church make little prayer pills that you can swallow in the morning?

Prayer, like love, takes time. But it is freely available, free like all the basic values of our life: music, poetry, the air that we breathe. And these are the things which build us up inside and constantly nourish us; they alone allow us to grow to be truly human. We would do well to recognize that we must give time to these values, to prayer, love, contemplation, dreaming so that we do not grow inwardly hard and rigid, and then pray only mechanically and love only artificially.

Only if we become aware of the living spring that we have can it refresh us and nourish us. Then our work will become much more productive, we shall be much more relaxed, will find it much easier to get on with people, smile more genuinely, and feel a warmer love. Why? Because we have spent half an hour in the morning with God, the source of our humanness.

If you have cloudy liquid which you want to make clear, stirring it with a spoon only makes things worse. What you have to do is leave the liquid for a while. Then the impurities sink to the bottom of the glass, and the water becomes clear and transparent. Some people say to me, 'Show me God! Prove that God exists.' I tell them to be patient. God is an experience to be had; they must calm down. 'Why?,' they ask. 'You'll see. God will reveal himself to you. I can't give you God on a plate; if he does not spring up from within you he is not the true God, but a word, an idea, an idol. God is a reality which springs up from the heart of our being and fills us. It's inexplicable. You just have to experience it. It's an experience you have to have, to have new every day. God is not given once for all; God is not proved once for all. Unless God is new every day, he is no longer God, but something else. God is always new, always being reborn.'

Prayer, too, must always be made all over again. And so must love. Louis Aragon remarked that human beings never acquire anything permanently.

Here are some remarks by the Greek Orthodox monk Metropolitan Anthony Bloom:

> You can only pray when you find yourself in the presence of God in a state of quietness and inner peace which transcends the notion of time. Here I don't mean our objectively measurable time, but our subjective experience of the passing of time around us and the certainty that we ourselves are timeless.

> If you embark on prayer, or love, or play, while at the same time looking at your watch, stop! Don't pray, don't make love, don't play. It's not worth it. When you begin to pray, take an alarm clock, set it to the time you want to devote to prayer and forget everything. It's like sleep: if you say 'I want to sleep just an hour', and look at your watch every five minutes, you won't sleep well. Like prayer, sleep is abandonment in which you lose all sense of time. All vital activities presuppose a forgetfulness of time, a forgetfulness of the clock.

Anthony Bloom goes on:

> We know what happens when we are on holiday. On holiday, there is nothing we need to do, even if we walk quickly, cheerfully and at a rapid pace, even if we run... We do not have the impression of being in a hurry, because what counts is the walk and not the destination.

> We need to learn to live as though we were always on holiday. You will tell me that that's impossible. Are you sure? Have you tried? I tell you that it *is* possible: I am always on holiday. That means that whatever I do, I do it as though I were on holiday. There is a way of walking when one is on holiday which does not necessarily consist in going more slowly, because I can walk fast, but without strain, without being in a hurry. There is a difference between being fast and rushing.

> Rushing is a source of tension, anxiety, whereas we can be fast while at the same time being calm and relaxed. In everyday life, I

do what I have to do without feeling time pressing. You may tell me that time does press. In that case I would reply that that is all the more reason to do what you have to do slowly, gently, calmly. Try putting on a dress or a shirt when you're in a hurry. What happens? The buttons come off, the dress tears, the shirt comes apart at the seams. You haven't gained any time, you've lost it. Try putting on your trousers or sweatshirt. What happens? You get your leg in the wrong hole and the sweatshirt is inside out. That shows that there is a rhythm to be found in existence: a holiday rhythm. That is the wisdom of time.

There is a great wisdom of time. And it is because we have not found it that we are anxious, tense, nervous, disturbed, neurotic, bad-tempered, aggressive. It would be so easy to live in a different way. And then what we do, we would do better. Much better and much quicker. For once you acquire this inner rhythm, this relaxation, this holiday rhythm, you end up treating everything as a game. My work's a game; my cooking's a game; my shopping's a game; my lecture's a game; this meeting is a game. Everything is a game. I'm always on holiday, I enjoy everything, I'm relaxed, and so I do it well.

Here's another suggestion of Anthony Bloom's:

Sit down and tell yourself: 'I'm doing nothing. I'm going to do nothing for five minutes.' Relax, and during this time repeat, 'I am in the presence of God, in the presence of my own self, in the presence of all the furniture around me. I am peaceful, not moving.'

I've tried that exercise and I can recommend it to you. I didn't have much time to pray one morning, and when I arrived at my desk around ten there was a pile of work: proofs to correct that would take days, a lecture to prepare for that very day in another city, lots of letters to write. So I said: first, I'm going to pray, to do nothing for quarter of an hour. I could have spent that quarter of an hour like a lion in a cage: nervous, tense, exasperated. But I told myself: 'You've quarter of an hour's holiday, quarter of an hour for yourself, to dream, to love.' So I lost fifteen minutes, from ten to ten-fifteen. It's difficult to tell you what I gained in that quarter of an hour. It was extraordinary. At 10.15 I began work, and all went well.

Try it! Try it when you're most tense, most wound up; when you've most to do. Say: 'I'm going to have five minutes off, five minutes' holiday.' You may say, 'That's crazy', but I assure you that it's wise. Spend the five minutes at the window. Open it and look at the sky, at the trees, at the birds, at whatever you can see. Take a few breaths of fresh air and look at nature. After five minutes you will find that the world is beautiful, and you'll be ready to start work. And it will go very well.

This necessary and healing time into which you sink so peacefully belongs to God. That's what Anthony Bloom tells us. He comments: 'The only real hindrance to prayer comes when you are buffeted by the tempest, when you let the tempest get inside you instead of letting it rage around you.' And he cites the example of the disciples in the boat with Jesus. Jesus was sleeping on a cushion, and the storm was raging around him. Little by little it entered the heart of the disciples, and they panicked. They woke Jesus, who said, 'Why are you disturbed?' And then he stood up and stilled the storm (Mark 4; Luke 8).

Never panic. The moment of an accident, when things are at their worst, is the time to relax, to take a deep breath, and to calm down. Real leaders are no more intelligent than others, nor more gifted than others, but they are people with a calm head and solid nerves. When the world is panicking, they say, 'No trouble, it will all get sorted out.' And then everyone calms down. The situation may indeed be serious, but that is why there's a need for calm. That's the only way in which problems can be solved.

In our twentieth century we are threatened by what is called stress. Panic situations are not just accidents, exceptional situations. All the time we are in a state of stress because of the rhythm of life, and we have constantly to tell ourselves to keep calm and not to panic.

Imagine a wheel constantly going round and round. If you're on the edge, you will go round with it. But if you get to the hub, the axle at the middle, what happens? Everything revolves around you, but you do not revolve; you stand firm. Prayer is precisely the act in which we rediscover our centre, our axis. The world revolves, people go crazy around you, but you can be like a mountain lake, still and calm.

Unfortunately many people nowadays have no centre, no direction, no head. They live on the circumference and not at the centre. But the whole secret of life is to find a centre and never to leave it. The ultimate aim of prayer is not just to give half an hour to the Lord. What counts is not this half-hour, but the action by which we set ourselves up at this centre in the morning and do not leave it for the rest of the day.

What I have tried to express in this chapter by reflecting on the time of loving, the time of listening, the time of living and the time of praying, is a certain way of existing, a certain life-style which establishes an attitude of mind that is prayer itself. Once it is acquired, this attitude steeps all that we do in a certain climate, and life becomes a game, poetry, liturgy. I like the word liturgy, because in the liturgy everything is done with calmness and dignity. To make my life a liturgy is to raise it to the level of celebration, of festival. When I eat, when I drink, when I am talking to someone, when I am walking, coming and going, everything must be done with a certain rhythm, a certain atmosphere, which will make my whole life radiate peace.

5   The Past Goes On

'The past is not dead. It is not even past'
(*William Faulkner*)

Remembering is a mysterious process! What are we doing when we remember, and what happens to us? Are those past hours or days completely obliterated or do they belong to dimensions which lose themselves unattainably and irrevocably in the dark depths of time? Or are they still tangible for us in some form; do they still have live in themselves? When we become preoccupied with our past, we say that we are losing ourselves in 'old' memories, 'old' times; the past seems 'old'. Is that the case? Has my past gone by like a clock, which I can never put back? In his extraordinarily rich book, entitled *Existence and Eternity*, which I have already mentioned, the French theologian Fernand Guimet answers this question in the negative:

> Memory is never a retrospect on the past, pure and simple. It is never a matter of restoring the past in its pastness. It does not perish with the event that gave it birth. It is a spiritual activity within us which, in the awareness of time that it gives us, is not in itself of the order of time. It escapes time by this power which it has to represent the past, i.e. to make it present, without telescoping or confusing the present with the past as it is grasped again by the memory, the past which we remember, in another dimension than that of pure temporality. One might say that memory is not *passé*. It simply allows the application of the past to all that it touches, to all that constitutes its object because it is within it. It simply recalls itself in a particular way, *sub specie aeternitatis*. By making the past present to us, it cannot but make it eternal. It is because within all our memories there is a beginning of eternal life that memory can be so valuable for us, indeed is priceless.

By memory, Guimet is saying, the past is renewed at the heart of the present, is realized in this present. Human beings have a special capacity to be able fully to recall a past event. We bring something up from the past, allow it to blossom again, give it a time in which to live and breathe. Guimet speaks of another dimension: there is more than the sphere of pure temporality, by which he means the general succession of moments of life which no one can cling on to, which escape us. He thinks that our recollection is not just a vigorous concern to recall things from the past; this activity in our minds takes place in the light of eternity. We eternalize the past by making it present.

Only memory is ultimately in a position to help us to understand the meaning and depth of an event, since we have to adopt a particular perspective and a degree of detachment if we are to decipher its meaning.

You will certainly be aware of all the discussions there are about the Gospel of John. It is said that this Gospel is not as historical as the other three. St John is criticized because instead of reporting events as they happened, he tends to interpret them, although he is always very precise in everything that he says. It is said that St John's Gospel is not historical, but an interpretation of the life of Christ, and therefore is not real history.

Now what is said of St John could also be said to a lesser degree of all the other Gospels. The Gospels are not stories about the life of Jesus, but the interpretation of these stories, at a certain distance which has been established between the event 'Jesus' and the moment at which the evangelists were writing. So it can be said that these writings are not historical because they are only memories, interpretations with all the distance which separates them from the time of the experiences that they contain. How does one reply? Is memory a betrayal of the event, or on the contrary is it a restoration of it at its deepest level?

Pick a particular event from your store of memories. For example, I might think of the moment of my religious vocation. I was sixteen years old; it was 8 May 1947, around three in the afternoon. I was reading a book, and for the first time the question occurred to me, 'Henri, why not become a priest?' This happening was a matter of no more than an hour. If I had described it the next day I couldn't have said much more, but I could have said more a month later and even more a year later. If you were to ask me about it now, nearly forty years later, I could write a book about it. This event, which did not take long, was clearly no minor matter in my young life. That hour was not an hour like thousands of others, but was deeply rooted in a very particular past, and soon took on a different dimension in terms of the future. The full significance of the message contained in this hour and all the events of our life, significance in a real and special sense, becomes evident only as one sets it in the context of everything that happened later. At that moment it comes alive and is linked to all the rest.

True history can only be written after a very great interval of time. One only becomes aware of the significance of a historical event when one can relate it to all that follows. Only from the time when one considers things in this perspective does light begin to fall on a past event, does it begin to speak to us, so that we recognize the way in which it fits into the web of existence.

St John is the evangelist who wrote his Gospel last. Matthew, Mark and Luke also wrote their Gospels at some remove from the life of Jesus, but perhaps the interval was not great enough. St John wrote his Gospel later. When the gospel had gone beyond the Palestinian and Jewish world, when it had penetrated the whole of the Mediterranean basin, when theological reflection had begun and developed from the first beginnings, the mystery of Jesus appeared in a new light, with new clarity. The Gospel of John is in a way much more historical than the other three, precisely because it has penetrated to the heart of the interpretation of three generations.

Memories reveal the truth of an event. And what is the Bible, if not a memory, a history? God does not reveal himself in a theology, a dogma or a creed, but in a history. History is revelation. If an Israelite child wanted to know who God was, he was not given a catechism with questions and answers; he was told stories, stories of God's dealings with men and women. You cannot really know people without knowing their history, and you cannot know about God without knowing about God's history.

As I give my lectures, when I look round the room, the faces I see are just blobs of colour. What do I know of the individual stories which underlie these blobs of colour? People do not know much about one another, because they do not know one another's stories. Those whom I have known personally for a long time become increasingly profound; they become 'more' and 'richer' for me, since they are now taking on depth. The superficial picture gradually gives way to time that we have spent together – their past. There can be no real knowledge without the dimension of memory. I only grasp that part of a being, that part of a thing which I can recall later; it is recollection which gives a being or an event the necessary consistency.

In the history of Israel, when people asked God for his name, God refused to give it to them. That means that God refuses to be fixed in a word. No word can express God. God is alive, and because God is alive, he only reveals himself in life. Penetrate the history of life, penetrate human history, penetrate the history of the chosen people, and you will find God. God is unfolded in a history. To know God is not to name him; to know God is to recall his mighty acts. In our French mass we sing the Great Hallel, Psalm 136, 'Give thanks to the Lord for he is gracious, and his love endures for ever...', which goes on to relate in a splendid series of verses the 'divine works' from creation to God's intervention in human history. All God's actions are named with gratitude and celebrated in a hymn.

We can see how in all this God discloses his face, reveals his personality, to make it accessible to us. It is by recollection that we are capable of discovering God. The Virgin Mary did precisely the same thing in her song of thanksgiving. The Magnificat (Luke 1.46-55) is a hymn of thanksgiving which takes up Psalm 136 in a denser, more concentrated form. And the Christian creed is similarly a recollection: a recollection of creation, incarnation, redemption, resurrection; a recollection of the whole of the life of Christ, the sending of the Holy Spirit and the history of the church. Here again, faith is expressed in history.

Those who read the Bible constantly ask, 'Who is this mysterious God who withholds his name from human beings and does not explain his actions, who leaves unanswered the human longing to get to know him?' They ask, 'How does God manifest himself in history? What being is acting there, and what attitude do we constantly see anew?' But readers of the Bible also want to see God at work in their own lives; they try to find God at times of meditation on the gospel. But you can do this in another way, by reading and meditating on the history of your own life.

I recently read somewhere that 'human beings are the best translation of the Bible'. This means that we really have two Bibles. The first is the history of a people, human history experienced in the transparency of the assured guidance of God; the second is our personal history, which we recall back to the earliest days of our childhood. People believe that the revelation of God is to be found in the first Bible, and that is right; but we also have our private Bibles in which we find the revelation of God addressed to us, and hear our word of God. This Bible is also important for us and infinitely rich in its own way: in it we recapitulate our own histories in order to find the trace of God in them, just as we do with the other Bible.

For me, the finest of all prayers is that in which I re-read my own life. Nowadays the term 're-read' is very much in vogue. One 're-reads' a past event and investigates its background. I also re-read my own life. What does it have to tell me? Try it yourself! Pick up your life, as you might pick up a book, and read it carefully page by page. Look in it for the significance of this or that event and personal experience, and go back as far as your memory takes you, right back to your childhood.

When I was four years old I was at a kindergarten in Alexandria; I can still see myself as that small boy. They had been showing us how to make little paper boxes, and suddenly for the first time I heard the chilling cries of the Muslim mourning women passing by the house on the way from a funeral. Standing on a chair, I was able to glimpse these uncanny figures, dressed in black veils, which seemed to me to be the heralds of the most fearful disaster. Even now I still have this vivid memory from childhood.

I can also picture the local playground. One day, a bigger boy than I, Simon M, pushed me headlong into a hole. I just missed an iron bar, which could have shattered my skull. I tell myself, 'Lord, you could have let me be killed at the age of four, but you saved me.'

Each of us can recall such events even after fifty years; each of us has this sort of experience. I could also faithfully depict less dramatic events than the two I have mentioned, memories from school, but they would not be of general interest. Yet how vivid such moments are! Every now and then what is supposed to be ordinary takes on an extraordinary dimension as a result of the depth of experience. So I re-experience my past with the devotion of a prayer, and in it have the spiritual experience of the presence of God. I recognize and feel that the Lord is here, the Lord is always present, in the depths of our consciousness and the ground of our being.

Now, in my fifties, I re-experience the past in quite a different, new way, and understand how my life is rooted in all that past, is immersed in it and draws on it, so that it all becomes prayer. When I take up my past history, it is not simply a memory for me, a vague nostalgic memory of my infancy. There is more than that: in memory there is more than memory, and in the past there is more than the past. And the story of my vocation, which I mentioned and which I could recount in detail, was an open window on the beyond; it was a climax to my existence.

When I want to find spiritual nourishment, I can open my Bible and meditate on the mighty acts of God with his people, the crossing of the Red Sea, and so on. But I can also open my own book, my own gospel, the story of my life, to wonder at the mighty acts of God with me, since I have my own history with the Lord.

There are two ways of looking at our past: the secular way which reduces life to a succession of flat and one-dimensional events, and the sacred way which sees in existence the secret and continuous act of God. Only the latter approach shows the basis and background to life and reveals its religious dimension, its dimension of eternity. My history then takes on meaning, acquires a particular savour, and my past becomes near, present, current.

What I can say of the course of my life, I can also say of the course of my day. How did I spend today? What has it shown me? What has it brought me? There are people who never have time to remember, to look back on their lives, to stand back and see all that has happened, what they have experienced – people with no depth-dimension. They live in the moment without ever emerging from it. Their life never reveals its meaning, and will never reveal God to them. We need to take time every evening to look back on our day, to weigh it up, to savour it and to discover those moments of grace in which God touched our heart, for in each one of those days there are moments, encounters, events which have marked and touched us.

There is no such thing as an 'empty' day, because no day in human life is without God's grace. There are all kinds of ways in which this can come to us, and it is the cause of particular insights and recognitions; it can be found in anything that has touched us. At the time these things happen I am not aware of their significance, and it is only afterwards, as a result of a certain distancing from them, that I can discover the particular flavour, the profound importance of such events.

What I was saying about St John could be applied to all of us.

Each day brings us a message. It is not a verbal message and cannot be put into words. It is a message which is perceived from the heart and kept in the heart. Remember the Gospel phrase about Mary: 'And Mary kept all these things and pondered them in her heart' (Luke 2.51).

We need to be capable of taking up our day, our existence, into our hearts. Remembering is bringing a past event into our hearts to give it new life. Language itself tells us this. In Latin, *recordare* means 'recall', and it is derived from the Latin word for heart: *cor, cordis*. We talk about a tape recorder. Language has a whole philosophy; it goes very deep. So recalling is not just an abstract activity of the brain, but a matter of the heart – and I would say that only the heart can recall fully. If only the traditional schools, both teachers and pupils, could understand that! What we call learning 'by heart' is nothing of the sort, because the heart is not involved at all; all that is involved is thought-mechanism. Language is understood wrongly and applied wrongly.

The heart is an organ which is capable of recall. In fact I can only remember what has gone through the depths of my heart. How long ago this happened is immaterial. But anything that leaves the heart uninvolved is soon forgotten, and ultimately becomes valueless, even if it was written only a short time previously. However, once it has reached my heart, it will become my flesh and blood, it will grow with me, become part of my inner self, part of my existence, will become my own self.

Seen in this way, my review of the day becomes a profound meditation, a way of perceiving God in my everyday life. That is what Mary is said to have done by keeping all these things in her heart; in that way she discovered the profundity of the mystery of Jesus. Having meditated on this for several decades she handed it on to St John, who had adopted her as his mother. The mystery of Jesus which passed through the heart of Mary also passed through the heart of St John. That is why the Fourth Gospel is so great and splendid a Gospel. It passed through two privileged hearts, the heart of Jesus' mother and that of 'the disciple whom Jesus loved...'

When saints want to write about God, they first of all look very carefully through their own lives. St Augustine's masterpiece is not his sermons, his homilies, nor even *The City of God*, but his *Confessions*, which are the story of his life, the web woven by God in his existence, the story of his quest for faith. In the

Confessions his life becomes a long invocation, a long conversation, a loving dialogue:

> Lord, do you remember my youth, when I was immersed in sin and I sought those delights which left me unsatisfied? Do you remember when my mother spoke to me and I did not listen? Do you remember when I finally felt your hand, which held me and guided me? Do you remember?

Deliberately to take up my own existence in the light of God is to embark on a dialogue, to discover a presence, the presence of the one who has followed me from the first moment of my conception to the present, the presence of the faithful companion who has taken me by the hand from the first moment of my life.

Later, in the sixteenth century, we have the memoirs of Peter Faber, a co-founder of the Jesuit order. He also set down his meditations on paper when he wanted to talk of God. He sought to demonstrate the guidance of God in his past. Nearer still, in the twentieth century, is the *Story of a Soul* by Thérèse of Lisieux, which is another set of reminiscences.

If you are suffering from spiritual aridity, instead of taking a theological or spiritual book, pick up a biography, the life of a saint. There you will find substantial nourishment, because in a biography it is the living God who speaks, whereas in theology we have a dead God. When you are talking to children you should always tell them stories, because it is through stories that they will understand, and not through concepts or ideas.

Above all, hang on to your personal memories, for they are something sacred. Modern men and women no longer have any roots; they continually move from place to place because of their work, constantly changing their homes, their cities and even their countries. In the United States people can live in as many as twenty different cities during their lives, and the same thing is beginning to happen in the Near East. There are people who have lived in Iraq, in Libya, in Saudi Arabia, in Kuwait, and so on. In this merry-go-round of modern life it is increasingly important to keep roots. In former times it was normal, natural, to have roots. People visited or lived in their ancestral home all their lives. Our old home in an area of Alexandria, where I spent my childhood, still exists, and naturally I stop and look at it every time I go past. The wall is falling down, the iron gate is rusting, but every window speaks to me, every step, and the two pillars to the right and left of the entrance. And the little garden. It all speaks to me of my childhood. We should all regularly make a pilgrimage to our roots, should return to our childhood homes, if not physically, at least by means of photographs, letters and mementoes. People may call this sheer nostalgia or sentimentality, but it is more than that. Certainly I am not excluding sentiment or nostalgia, but it can be given another depth, another dimension.

Those who are of my age may remember a sentimental French song which went, 'Memories, memories, sweet and tender, of happiness which seems almost forgotten'. And then it goes on: 'Memories, memories, the past cannot die as long as it remains a memory in our hearts.'

Certainly the past cannot die, and memories keep this past alive, present. That is why memories are so sacred. Human beings are their past. I am my own past. What I am now is what has been formed slowly over the years. I am a tree with concentric circles, and each passing year has made its mark deep within me. I am a pyramid built up of layer upon layer, the result of my infancy, my education, my family, my religious training, my travels, and so on. All this crystallizes around the small being that I am; all this has shaped me, made me, formed me. My being is my past; I am my past; that is why it does not pass.

The slightest past event has shaped us in a particular way, has marked us for ever; that is why it is part of our eternity. We shall always be what we have been, what we have experienced, what we have felt. And all that will one day rise again and be eternally alive.

One day I reminded my mother of a journey we had made to Lebanon in 1944. I told her that all its happy memories, the villages which we had gone through, the events that we had experienced, would never pass away, but were inscribed in God's eternity. The journey would last for ever. For me, access to eternity consists in passing through the gate of death to rediscover a concentration of our lives on the other side. There we shall experience all the fullness of the eternal past. One day all our events will lie before us like an open book, like a present reality. The past will come alive again. Nothing passes away, nothing disappears, but all is gathered together in God's great storehouse. If God is eternal, and if we become eternal with him, it is in order to rediscover in him all our past life, no event of which can disappear.

That is an extraordinary hope for me, for each of our relationships, each of our friendships, each of our loves is more than an unforgettable story, an inestimable treasure. One of the most important messages to hand on to people is the message of hope and trust:

> All that you have experienced is of value, is important, is serious – so serious that God preserves it and gathers it together. And one day he will say to you: 'You have not just lived your life in the past, but you will live it always. It will be yours, you will take it up again in the eternal light of the beyond, but with quite a different clarity, quite a different density.'

That's marvellous! You may call it wishful thinking, but I would reply that that is just not true. If a stone, a simple stone, can exist for billions of years without decaying, would you want something that is infinitely richer, infinitely more important than a stone, to disappear one day completely? If God can preserve a simple small stone for billions and billions of years, is he going to delete the whole of my past existence at a stroke? No, this spiritual existence is there for ever: it has been, it is, and it will be.

None of it is ephemeral. Nothing is ephemeral for anyone who lives his or her life at this level. However, here the question arises: 'At what level?' Look at this diagram of a cone. You can live your life at the base, in the middle, or at the point. It is at the point that everything is concentrated, that everything is eternal. The point is my real being, my essential being, which does not pass away.

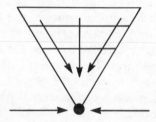

It is at that level that all my life is concentrated; it is there that it will be taken up and kept for ever. That is where eternity is. To be eternal is not to perpetuate oneself in the final state one has reached, i.e. a human ragamuffin at the end of life. I am not interested in perpetuating myself as an old man; that is not eternity.

What is capable of living at this level is a force. I do not have the strength of my body, but the strength of my life. Those who concentrate all their past in the present moment are not simply the human beings that they are now but human beings with all the irresistible thrust of their past. That is a way of living in a state of synthesis, of totality. If I only live as I am now, I am only the thinnest of films on the surface of my being. But if I live with all the weight and all the thrust of what I have been, my life takes on quite a different dimension. Those who remember are those who have given all the weight of what they have been to their existence.

There is such richness, such fullness, in our past, that it would be a pity to live only in the passing moment, the fleeting instant, without devoting to it all of our past lives. In other words, I can experience the instant uniquely on the surface of the cone, but I can also involve the whole pyramid in the present act and make it bear the whole weight of my past existence on the point of the cone, here and now.

The word that I speak, the act that I venture, can be the concentration and sum of all my past. At that moment living becomes a total act of all being. There is extraordinary power there. But to avoid misunderstandings, there are some things that we should remember.

By eternity I do not mean holding on to our final state, which is what some people are afraid of: the sorry end of our existence. Who of us would be happy if we supposed that we would go on for ever as an old man or woman? No, eternity is something quite different. When Mary appeared to St Bernadette at Lourdes, she had the attractive appearance of a girl of about fifteen. According to historical tradition, Mary died in Ephesus as an old woman of eighty-five. So among other thing Lourdes is a sign to us that human beings continue for ever in the best form that they had on earth, and that the rest of their lives will be absorbed by this form, which illuminates and supplements them from within.

What will we look like in the life to come? That is a question which crops up again and again. What impression will we make there? Don't worry. You will look as you did in the prime of life, and will not reflect any stage of your bodily decline. The resurrection body will reveal the best of you; the highpoint of your existence will be raised to true life; it will blossom, develop fully and be brought to full maturity. Possibly this new appearance will not be immediately recognized by others, but it will be our true face, since we shall be living with God in the truth. Our eternal appearance is the appearance of our youth in the higher sense, our true youth, and that means that it will be the appearance of our deepest being.

Anyone who already lives and breathes this vision becomes a source of power for others. I am not the power of my body but the power of my being and the life that I live. Those who integrate their past into the present moment and concentrate it there are made up not only of the human nature which is visible at a particular moment, but of more: at the same time they embody the whole inner drive of their past. There is an art of living in a state of synthesis, in a state of totality.

By contrast, if I see only what I am now, I am no more than a tiny speck on the surface of my being. But if I live with all the weight and all the impetus of what I have been, I shape my life in quite a different way, and it takes on another dimension. Those with good memories at every moment give their existence another dimension by holding on to their previous experience. What reveals the meaning of the present is a reference to particular events which were experienced intensively at some point in the past.

Here is an example. Last time I was in the church of St Joseph in Cairo I spent the whole of mass watching a mother and her child in front of me. The child was standing on the edge of the pew, and the mother had her arms around the child while it was swinging, walking, and so on. Every now and then she would put it on the ground. The child did what it wanted, and all the time the mother carefully kept an eye on it. She was praying, but she never let the child out of her sight. It could have fallen a hundred times during the mass, but never did. At the last moment, the mother, by a tiny movement, would catch the child or hold it back by its coat. You might say that I was watching the child instead of praying. But it was my best prayer! The whole mass was a marvellous contemplation of the love of God.

This small incident is in the past, but it is now present for ever and has become a point of reference for me. This trivial event, which I experienced deeply in my heart, is the catalyst for quite a new experience in this sphere. Just looking at a mother carrying a child or holding its hand brings back memories of that other experience in church to produce quite a different feeling and quite a different depth. Memory feeds the present and fills it with incomparable riches. There is a richness of life in our past, a richness of expression, which it would be a pity to leave on one side. This richness can be with us all the time and become nourishment, delight, enjoyment. That is what memory is.

Memories nourish our present with their savour and their fire, and they fill us with inestimable value. So we should not regard our wealth of experiences as museum-pieces and leave them lying unused, but should deliberately make active use of them. That is what I understand by the spiritual activity of recollection.

Old people are those who have this wisdom of memory. An old person is someone who remembers, and that is splendid. You might say that this is a waste of time, but I would reply that it is the most important thing for old people: remembering for themselves and remembering for others. There is a wisdom, an intensity of life in memories. Memory is never an empty experience, but something full, something which plunges its roots into the heart of existence.

I said earlier that human beings are their past. But what past? The individual past or the eternal past? Science shows me that my past is not only my own past but the past of all the earth and of all humanity; it puts down its roots very, very wide and very, very deep. My past is the world of minerals and the world of vegetables, the world of animals and the human world; my past is most deeply rooted in the earth and in the centuries.

I bear within myself all this history of the universe and of humanity. When people say in scientific, technical terms that ontogenesis recapitulates phylogenesis, they mean that the history of the individual recapitulates that of the species. The little embryo in its mother's womb undergoes in nine months the stages undergone by the whole of life over its evolution. If you analyse your body, you will find in an infinitesimal form the ninety-two elements which exist in nature. Human beings are microcosms; each body is a concentration of the universe.

When I make contact with the earth, I make contact with myself and remember my past. That we experience such an attraction to earth is not simply a result of gravity; it is because there is a profound relationship between human beings and the earth. I am a son of the earth and the earth is my mother. I come from it, because it bore me and it is my own past. The tree is my past, the plant is my past, the flower is my past, the forest is my past. I have been that way before; we have all been that way.

We feel the same thing in the proximity of animals. The affection and the attachment that we feel for animals is not just sentimentalism; there is a profound affinity between them and us. We are made of the same stuff, we are brothers and sisters, we are one. The creaturely world forms one family because we have one past. What is modern genetics concerned with? What is heredity? It is this being moulded by experiences which extend far back in time. That is what Lamarck's theory about the transmission of acquired characteristics is all about. All the experiences of flowers, birds, cats, apes and so on in the past have been stocked up, accumulated in certain cells, and have been constantly transmitted over millions of years to make us what we are today. We are the result of this long past, this long earthly history. Evolution is ineradicably inscribed upon us and we bear it with us. Heredity is the memory of our species, the recollection of the whole cosmic ascent towards us.

Education is akin to this; it is the reappropriation by each child in a few years of all the past experience of humankind. Everything that has been experienced and thought between Adam and Einstein, all the work of discovery and knowledge by the peoples of antiquity, the philosophy of Plato and Aristotle, the thoughts of St Thomas and Hegel, all the philosophers, sages and poets, are presented to the child on a plate from which he or she can help themselves. It is a gift of past humankind, a memento of all generations, an everlasting present, for the young person to take.

But how is a child to remember all this with enjoyment, by heart and with heart? There is an art in relating history well. Unfortunately this art is all too often reduced to broad, superficial knowledge and the hasty transmission of dates and synoptic tables of facts. But that is not history or remembering. History has to become a story, a true story: 'Once upon a time...' At that moment the child listens and the story enters into its heart. Relating history is an art. There are many history teachers, but very few of them have mastered it so that they know how to make the past live again, make the heart of their pupils beat faster.

Thus through evolution, through heredity, through education, little by little, we inherit a whole primal wealth which slowly becomes ours. To remember ourselves is to take possession of this priceless treasure.

What is an educated person? Not someone who has knowledge but someone who has roots. For many people culture is often no more than an accumulation of knowledge, an encyclopaedic mind; a culture person is thought to be someone capable of saying everything there is to be said about a subject, or something about everything, depending on what it is... Such a person is a walking dictionary; but we don't need walking dictionaries because we now have electronic brains which work much better. Rather, an educated, cultivated person is someone who lives with all the past generations, who lives with all the humanity of former days, and who lives with all the wisdom of the ancients, who puts roots down into the world of yesterday and today. The aim of education is to transfer into myself the universal human being, to become this person of all other times and all other places, thanks to the memory of the heart.

The memory of the heart allows us to experience love between one another. We find ourselves back in a common past. What is a culture? What is a civilization? What is a nation? A nation is not a countryside; a countryside is a geographical entity: mountains, valleys, rivers, frontiers. But a nation is rather different: it is a common past, a common history, common experiences.

What is Alexandria? Alexandria is all these faces, a quite specific mentality, different from that of Cairo, different from that of Upper Egypt, different from that of Lebanon, different from that of France. It is a mixture of all these things at once and it is also something else. There is a distinctive culture in Alexandria, a distinctive civilization and mentality, a very special spirit. It is the shared past of shared experience which helps us to communicate, to feel at ease with one another; there is a family spirit. At national level, at the level of a city or a village, there is this sharing of past experiences which are our riches, which are our power of communication.

To end with I would like to demonstrate that all this is not a collection of ideas, theories, dreams; it has an existential dimension. Some years ago, when I was lecturing on death, I raised this question:

What is the past of humankind?
Where are the dead to be found?
Where are those who have preceded us? What is their abode?
In heaven? In hell? In purgatory? In limbo? With God?
With the devil? Where are they?

I replied to these questions by saying that there is in fact only one humanity, the humanity of today, here and now.

When I was small, after my grandmother had died, my mother told me that she was now in heaven. I wanted to take a long, long ladder and climb up to my grandmother. Since then, I've come to realize that I don't need a long ladder, for our dead, those who have gone before us, are there – there in me, in you, in us, here and now. There is no other world than our own; there is no other universe than our own; there is no heaven anywhere above, and no hell anywhere below. What exists is today's humanity, which bears within it the humankind of former times as a mother carries her child in its womb. We are the summing up of all former humankind: we are its living and present memory. Our present existence bears this fruit, hundreds of thousands of years old, which the earth has slowly brought forth.

More than twenty years ago I wrote this, about death as a restoration and a return to earth:

Death is the moment at which each of us flows back into the great stream of life from which we emerged. This reintegration is not a dissolution into the anonymous but an ascent into the personal; it is not a return to primal energy but a transcending of ourselves in love; it is not a return to the timeless but an entry into eternity; it is not a matter of being consumed, but an ascent; it is not sinking into the unconscious but an ecstasy of the superconsciousness; it is not destruction but realization.

Then the dead begin to be active. They attach themselves to the living and give them additional life. The dead do not withdraw into a sphere of the universe outside the earth, to lead a life there among their like, but through every act of their dying they find themselves restored to the flow of life which gave birth to them.

The dead now experience an intensification of their present. Their death does not take them away from us, but makes them intimately near to us, and this nearness is many times more definitive than it could ever have been before.

In their spiritual power they become a ferment for those of us who are alive. Through the presence of the dead, human society raises itself step by step and will one day find its fulfilment. The dead are the motive power of development and all progress. Through them evolution slowly makes its way through time towards its goal.

The other world is within this world; the beyond is here. Former humankind adds itself to humankind today through the great reintegration of death, by the restoration of the dead. Present humankind is none other than a summation of all the human beings who have ever lived. We bear in ourselves the living but concealed presence of all the human beings of the past.

Each of us is supported by the whole line of his or her ancestors. This is not symbolic, figurative language, but a real ontological fact. All the dead are really alive, and they continue to live in us.

My dead live in my heart, in my body and blood; they live my life with me. I recapitulate them, I am their last word, they speak through me, they work in me, they remain active in me as the ongoing past which is the present – in all of us, in each of us.

So there exists in us and in today's humankind a sort of pressure from within, the pressure of all past generations waiting to see what we will make of them, what we will do with this world from which they too came forth, which they know. They confidently whisper, 'Take over the baton, take up the succession, take on the task.' We are responsible for a world which was entrusted to us by others. Are we acting accordingly?

There is only one humanity and there is only one human person who has existed over the millennia of history. I am, we are, this person. To the degree that we are inwardly watchful, sensitive and responsive to the inner call of all those who preceded us, this recollection of all that is past will bear fruit – not just for me or you, but for the whole human species. If we notice any progress in humankind, then we also note the reason: its good memory.

What I said about inheriting, which is quite simply the accumulation of experiences from the past in the mechanisms of memory made up of genes and chromosomes, I am now also saying about humanity in its spiritual and ontological dimensions. In our spirits, in our bodies, in our hearts, in our consciousness and our sub-consciousness, we experience this irresistible thrust of all the past generations who are expecting from us the fruition that they have a right to expect. This fruition will be the new humanity which must come to birth in us one day 'when the times have been fulfilled', when human beings have reached their full maturity and stature.

Once we have arrived at this final point, this omega point, the whole of past history will be actualized for ever in eternity. Heaven is only this eternal moment of remembering again all that we have been, all that we have experienced in the presence of God.

6 The Redemption of Time

'I am worth more than my life'
(*A young man before execution*)

After I had given a lecture on the theme discussed in the previous chapter, one of those present was quite disturbed and came up to me: 'Father, you say that the past does not pass. As far as I'm concerned, that's a terrible prospect. My life is a series of mistakes, an ongoing tragedy, and in heaven I wouldn't want to find that I had to begin that all over again...'

I told myself that she was right. For those who have had a happy childhood it is good that the past does not pass, but I can understand how those whose life has been one long *via dolorosa* can say to themselves, 'My God, no... Please make the past past, let this nightmare disappear, so that I can at last turn the page and forget...'

That is precisely the problem I want to deal with in this chapter, which I have called 'The Redemption of Time'. I could also call it 'Obliterating the Past'. So does that mean transitoriness?

In no circumstances should the concept of an everlasting past be understood in terms of a retrospective destiny which takes our breath away and weighs heavily upon us. However, to some people the past evidently seems to be an eternal destiny which ties and binds them to what was, to what they can no longer change, to their failures in life, or to what has gone very wrong. Suffering gnaws at them, and they ask themselves, 'Are we helpless? Can we never break loose from this chain, break out of this darkness, to reach a freer, clearer sphere in which we can pick up again the whole of the life that we have lived and come to grips with it afresh, so that we can put many things right, make up for what we have not done and rescue what we have lost?' Is there no magic formula for what Marcel Proust called 'the search for lost time', for the work to which he gave this title seems to recapitulate his whole life in time? But what is the meaning of the redemption of time? What is making good? What is the redemption of the past?

In a famous text, Nietzsche contemplates with furious rage and despair this past against which he feels impotent, this past which is beyond his grasp and which escapes him. Nietzsche, the one who based all his philosophical work on the will-to-power of the superman who can overcome his destiny, comes up against the wall of the past, which raises itself before him like an insuperable obstacle. He says:

> To redeem the past, and to transform every 'It was' into 'I wanted it thus' – that alone do I call redemption.

These lines from his *Thus Spoke Zarathustra* inspired me to the title of this chapter. So we shall now try to see the meaning of the redemption of the past and whether this redemption is truly possible.

> 'It was': that is what the will's teeth-gnashing and most lonely affliction is called. Powerless against that which has been done, the will is an angry spectator of all things past.
>
> The will cannot will backwards; that it cannot break time and time's desire – that is the will's most lonely affliction.
>
> It is sullenly wrathful that time does not run back: 'That which was' – that is what the stone which it cannot roll away is called.
>
> And so, out of wrath and ill-temper, the will rolls stones about and takes revenge upon him who does not, like it, feel wrath and ill-temper.
>
> Thus the will, the liberator, becomes a malefactor: and upon all that can suffer it takes revenge for its inability to go backwards.
>
> This, yes, this alone is *revenge* itself: the will's antipathy towards time and time's 'It was'.
>
> Can there be redemption when there is eternal justice? Alas, the stone 'It was' cannot be rolled away: all punishments, too, must be eternal! Thus madness preached. No deed can be annihilated; how could a deed be undone through punishment? That existence too must be an eternally-recurring deed and guilt, this, this is what is eternal in the punishment 'existence'!

These thoughts of Nietzsche's are fearful. No act can ever be undone, and everything lasts for ever. That is also suggested by the title of a novel by Paul Bourget, *Our Deeds Follow Us*. That phrase contains a terrible obsession, a feeling of fright and anguish in the face of this ineluctability of an action which, once performed, follows us and pursues us indefinitely. Even punishment, says Nietzsche, cannot do away with the fact that the action has been performed. It is there as a curse.

All 'It was' is a fragment, a riddle, a dreadful chance – until the creative will says to it: 'But I willed it thus!' Until the creative will says to it: 'But I will it thus! Thus shall I will it.'

Here in a strange way Nietzsche attempts to do away with this fatality of the past by proclaiming in the attitude of a philosopher: 'Yes, that is basically what I wanted. I failed, but basically I wanted that to happen. I am not in a position to obliterate the past, and so I explain it to myself in a different way and tell myself that this is really how I wanted it, how I want it now and how I shall want it in the future.'

But in acting in this way I am fooling myself. This Stoic attitude is no solution, for the will always comes up against the wall of time, the wall of the past, without being able to cross it.

This leads us to reflect on the significance of the feeling of guilt. Here I would refer particularly to a remarkable book by a contemporary French philosopher Jean Lacroix, *The Feeling of Guilt*. Lacroix distinguishes between two different, not to say opposed, attitudes: remorse and repentance.

I have done something bad, a wicked act that I regret. But this regret can take two forms: either remorse or repentance. For most of us, these two words are equivalent and almost synonymous. To say that 'I feel remorse' or 'I repent' seems to us to be two ways of saying the same thing. But in fact here we have two feelings which are not only different, but diametrically opposed to each other.

Remorse is a useless and ineffective regret which consists in wishing that the fault had not happened and suffering from one's inability to suppress it. Men and women torment themselves inwardly, saying, 'Oh, if only I had not done that! Oh, if only that could never have been! Oh, what a shame that it happened!...' And in so doing they shut themselves up in a vicious circle of useless regrets.

There is a proverb which goes, 'Too late is too late.' Those who are eaten away by remorse are undermined within by a feeling which gnaws at them and consumes them, by a kind of morbid and unhealthy anguish which devours them. Then follows self-condemnation in hopeless questions about guilt, for within the feeling of guilt there is the rejection of whatever has been done and its condemnation by our conscience.

Do you ever notice the spontaneous gestures which people make when they suddenly become aware of a mistake, gestures which you yourself also make? The hand goes to the forehead, the fist hits the table or the wall, someone claps her hands, someone tears his hair or beats his breast. Remarkable reactions! What do they mean? They mean that we want to punish ourselves: we chastize ourselves, we take vengeance on ourselves. Do you know that beating the breast goes back to the time of the desert fathers? In order to satisfy their need for repentance, they would pick up a stone and hit themselves on the chest with it, very hard. This gesture survives down to the present day in our mass. Our fingers gently touch our chests when we say – unfortunately more or less mechanically – the confession:

I confess that I have failed to do good and done evil. I have sinned in thought, word and deed through my fault, my own fault, my grievous fault.

However, mild though it has become, our gesture of self-punishment still expresses the same thing – a need for atonement. People think that they can atone for their guilt by pain and punishment, and it is here that Nietzsche strikes. Stubbornly and desperately he describes those who grind themselves down in sick anxieties and meaningless self-accusations; he knows how useless the whole exercise is: too late is too late. This behaviour comes near to masochism: masochism has many dimensions, but one of them is the spiritually painful feeling of guilt which one continues to nurture. Guilt feelings can take on morbid forms, even extending to a delight in moral pain, which people carefully preserve by constantly savouring their misery all over again. Here the sufferers persuade themselves that their suffering is good and redemptive in itself. But it is only good and redemptive to the degree that it has a meaning, brings with it faith, confidence and love.

A person suffering from remorse may seem to be an embittered being, but this bitterness is disguised; in a veiled way it seeks to give the impression that God finds pleasure in this suffering of the conscience. We all know from our childhood days that spirituality of sorrow which sought to convince us, 'The more you suffer, the greater is God's joy.' It is precisely at this point that Sigmund Freud's famous concept of the 'sadistic father' comes in – a God who takes pleasure in human suffering. This phenomenon can go so far as to become an obsession, a form of neurosis consisting in the compulsive repetition of an action, as though those in its grip were driven by inner shadows which did not allow them any rest.

Another type of neurotic and obsessional act is the scruple, which is also associated with remorse. Pushed to extremes, the scrupulous attitude can bring about the most disturbing form of neurosis, which is called manic depression or melancholy: in ordinary language, a nervous breakdown. Here lies one of the dangers of self-examination, which for many people consists in going over the past time and again in a sterile way, so that it becomes a source of discouragement and bad conscience: a more or less obsessional mental rumination which paralyses and raises obstacles. Remorseful people feel steeped in their failure, imprisoned in a enclosed world from which they cannot escape, plunged into a morass, all the time arguing with themselves and shutting themselves in. They normally end up in despair and even suicide.

Remember Judas! He felt his guilt penetrating his whole being, fettered and imprisoned by this past hour of betrayal; he could no longer see a future; his past became a future which had nothing else in view but his own guilt. As the psalm puts it, 'For I acknowledge my misdeeds, and my sin is ever before me' (Ps.51.5).

So people's lives can come to an inner standstill, since they experience not only their past but also their future as past, as they are caught in the past. For what is life, if not constant new departures and inward rejuvenation, a new flourishing in the power of eternal resurrection? However, those who are torn apart by remorse are incapable of all that. Their wings seem broken; it is as though they have stopped real life and put themselves outside it. In banishing themselves they recognize themselves as victims of their guilt, fettered to the past, over which Nietzsche laments, having made the unchangeable past a rigid time which eternalizes itself for them.

Let us look more closely at that Christian spirituality of past days which has celebrated grief. Nietzsche could help us to understand Sartre's analyses of God as the spy whose eye is fixed permanently on men and women to torment them. For Sartre a look is that which fixes someone or something. To look at someone or something is to fix it in an immovable image, to transform it into a 'statue of salt', to make a new Lot. Those who suffer remorse look at themselves and at the same time they feel that they are being looked at, since there is a close relationship beween these two attitudes. In looking at oneself, one feels one is also being looked at by others and by God, and this look is at the same time condemnation, a definitive judgment without any appeal.

Victor Hugo wrote a famous poem about conscience, from which I quote a few lines:

> When with his children, clothed in animal skins,
> dishevelled, livid, in the midst of tempests,
> Cain fled before Jehovah...

Having killed his brother, devoured with remorse, Cain flees the implacable gaze of God, across plains, mountains and valleys, steppes and forests. Every time he looks back, he sees this gaze fixed on him. He hides in the depths of his tent, but the gaze is always there. He asks to be buried alive in order to escape the terrible vision. The earth slowly covers the body, the neck, the eyes, the head, down to the last hair. When it was all finished,

> The eye was in the tomb and looked on Cain.

Today we shudder at such a story of God, at such a view of God: God as a spy, a police inspector, an inquisitor, whose gaze follows us step by step, whom nothing escapes. In some churches this eye looks down from the ceiling with a vividness one cannot miss, a wide open eye which sees absolutely everything. Is it surprising that such an image of God inevitably also prompts a tendency towards atheism? Here is how Sartre relates an experience from the time of his adolescence:

> God sees me, I feel his gaze within my head and my hands, horribly visible, a living target. Indignation saved me: I was furious at so gross an indiscretion, I blasphemed, I murmured as against my grandfather: Holy name of God, name of God. He will never look at me again.

Sartre's atheism is precisely the rejection of this inquisitive look which violates human intimacy and in the process deprives it of all liberty. God sees me, so I am not longer free. Moreover, this impalpable look, anonymous and omnipresent, is like the unification of all human looks, the regard of all spaces infiltrating into the human heart.

For Sartre, God is a 'voyeur' in the sense that contemporary psychology gives to this word. God is the one who tries to see through the keyhole what is going on in my room, what is going on in my heart. God is inquisitiveness itself. At the same time as God fixes human beings in their past, he also fixes them in their bodies, which are also their past. What is our body? Our body is not ourselves; it is only a certain image of ourselves. It is our past rather than our future; our animal nature rather than our humanity. It is that by which we participate in the animal world, the material world; that which does not have the possibility of changing from one day to the next, despite all the make-up. A woman keeps the face she has. An old man will never succeed in making himself a child's face.

This look, then, by fixing us in our past, becomes a kind of death sentence for us.

Nietzsche is the one who is mostly behind this. He is the one who has principally prompted analyses of the regard of God. In his book *The Gay Science*, he tells of a young girl in the bath. Her mother says to her, 'God sees everything'. The girl's reaction is, 'How indecent! What right has he to see me in my bathroom?'

At another point Nietzsche cites the example of Judas, on whom Jesus looked twice – at the last supper and at his betrayal. At the supper he gave Judas a piece of bread and looked at him – knowing all – with the words, 'What you do, do quickly' (John 13.27b). Then, when he approached Jesus to betray him in the garden of Gethsemane, Jesus looked on him again and said, 'Judas, do you betray the son of man with a kiss?' (Luke 22.48). For Nietzsche, the motive for this betrayal was Jesus' look. This intolerable gaze had to be extinguished, and that meant the death of Jesus.

Now let us look at Nietzsche's Zarathustra.

On his journey, Zarathustra encounters the desolate, terrifying valley called 'Serpent's Death' and there encounters the ugliest man, Judas. Judas discloses to him the true cause of his crime:

Zarathustra! Zarathustra! Read my riddle! Speak, speak! What is the revenge on the witness?
But he – had to die: he looked with eyes that saw everything –

he saw the depths and abysses of man, all man's hidden disgrace and ugliness.

His pity knew no shame: he crept into my dirtiest corners. This most curious, over-importunate, over-compassionate god had to die.

He always saw me: I desired to take revenge on such a witness - or cease to live myself.

The god who saw everything, even man: this god had to die. Man could not endure that such a witness should live.

So Judas commits two murders which cannot be separated from each other: the murder of Jesus, aimed at destroying this look which he cannot stand; and his own murder, his suicide. The two go together, and in this double murder of Judas lies the proof of what I affirmed earlier: remorse brings condemnation of self by self, of self by others and of self by God. Judas did not simply suppress Jesus' gaze on him, for this gaze would have pursued him beyond death. No, to get rid of it he had to do away with himself. 'The eye was in the tomb and looked on Cain.' God has to exist. His eye burns in the midst of the human person and sees all. For man to live, God must die.

These interpretations shake us, since they reveal a real tragedy of misunderstanding. So let us now pass to rather brighter perspectives and speak of repentance.

What is repentance? It, too, is the recognition of personal guilt, but at the same time it goes beyond it and overcomes it.

Repentance seeks to by-pass the past by looking forward, by looking to the future.

Remorse directs us towards the past. Repentance projects us towards the future.

So there is a world of difference between the two. The idea of redemption and restoration by means of a particular action is an integral part of the concept of repentance. Here we are not held eternally captive in the past, but are given the possibility of going beyond it. That is the marvellous good news we are given. In the end, nothing is ultimately lost and there is never occasion for total despair. Everything can be taken up again and fundamentally reshaped; everything can be blotted out or purified. Everything can rise again in purity.

That sounds incredible, unbelievable. Nevertheless, the good news to men and women is indeed that there is no death.

There is no death. Not in any form. It is wrong to think of death as final defeat and the utmost unhappiness for men and women. This view is false: it lacks reality, it has no existence, because the new element in this world news which has reached us is the redemption of human beings and the redemption of time. It is the news of our future which discloses itself to us and leads us to brighter realms of life. It is the news of the liberation of men and women from all time, so that they do not remain indissolubly entangled in the mistakes which they made in the past. It is the news of the redemption of men and women from a guilty past.

But what does that amount to in practice? How are we to justify what I have just said? Can one reach back into the past and destroy seed and crops there, make something as though it had never happened?

The answer is yes and no. In fact this is impossible, since what has happened has happened. But one can extinguish the past in oneself as a conscious human action, and it is on this spiritual level that redemption takes place. The tangible fact is the physical or psychological consequence of a completed action. This consequence is irreversible. It belongs to the past. If I break a precious vase, once the vase is broken there is nothing that can make it not broken. The deed is done, and the fact itself cannot be destroyed, cannot be suppressed.

But the action which underlies the fact, which is its meaning, its moral and spiritual significance, its profound and internal motivation, can always be modified, up to the point of death, by a change in my inner attitude, by a transformation in the depths of my being.

Let me explain.

Our life is made up of a succession of actions: this act, followed by another, then by a third, a fourth, and so on. But over and beyond this succession of actions there is the person who dominates them. This person, who stands above them, at the top of the cone, at the point of the pyramid, transcends the successive actions which he or she performs, transcends the unfolding of his or her life, transcends the flow of time. It is because human beings are, to a degree, beyond time, because they already belong to eternity, that they are capable of taking up the past, not by transforming a fact but by a spiritual reworking of their action at the level of consciousness. A fact may be a past reality, but the action which lies at its origin is not. It remains deep within me, and that is why it is capable of being taken up again, of being remade, of being recreated.

That is what I understand by repentance. Repentance is taking up an action at an intentional level. In regretting my past action I deny it, and by doing so the self which is at the source of this act takes up this past to suppress it. In other words, the significance of the past always depends on the future. It is precisely because human beings are beyond time that they are not eternally the prisoners of their past. So the question is not that of knowing what our past is, but of knowing what we want to do with it.

Here is an illustration. When you go by train from Cairo to Alexandria, in Mustafa Pasha you pass a vast dump belonging to the Chekat El Nahas steelworks containing enormous piles of all kinds of old automobiles, old corrugated iron, old boxes, all the metal of Alexandria rusting in the open air. All this debris of the past is taken by the factory, put in a furnace and transformed into glowing new ingots of steel. What this firm constantly does with its old iron, human beings can do with their own lives and their past. The problem is not to know what our past is, but to know what we are going to do with it, what we want to do with it. I can look sadly at all these rusty old sheets of corrugated iron, all these carcasses of cars put on the junk heap and say, 'What a pity, what a catastrophe!' That is how some people contemplate their past.

But on the other hand I can look at all the used, rusted, twisted past and say to myself, 'I am capable of transcending all this, remaking it, remoulding it, letting it flow into something new, recreating myself in a new being. Human beings can constantly remake themselves, time and again.' That is the good news, that is hope, that is joy, that is 'the redemption of time'.

The history we have to make delivers us from the history that we have made, and repentance delivers us from the determinism of the past. By 'determinism' I mean all the force hidden in the laws of physics, that is, the inevitability with which one phenomenon succeeds another and simply ends up at a predestined goal, inscribed in advance in the pattern of its unfolding. There is the determinism of the force of gravity, the determinism of falling bodies, and so on.

But human beings are capable of transcending what determines them if they plunge deeply enough into themselves, to the level of their essential being, their person. They can take up their past action and as it were remake it, reshape it. The German philosopher Max Scheler knew where the roots of action lie, and in particular he knew that they can be destroyed:

Seize the fault, once recognized, by the roots, to eradicate it from the person and give oneself the freedom to do good.

The very meaning of the past is transformed by repentance, which is not simply repair of the past but transformation of the past. What is the difference between these two words?

Suppose I have an old pan with two holes in it. I go to the *sankari* (an Arab word which means tinsmith) and ask him to put two small patches on the holes. I get back home, and put the pan on the stove, but soon the holes develop again. I go back to the man for another repair. After about two weeks I have to go through the whole process all over again. It's always the same with repairs. If you have an old automobile, and put a spare part in here, a piece of wire there, the automobile may go for a while, but it will soon stop again. That means more tinkering about; the process never ends. That's the trouble with repairs.

If redeeming time, redeeming human beings, were like doing repairs, the prospect would be pretty grim. I don't need someone to repair my past; I need someone to transform me – and to transform is to recreate.

Transformation is a total remaking, a radical remaking – not a bit of patchwork, a botched-up repair. It is believing that my life can be taken up anew, that I can remake a child's heart for myself.

'Give us, Lord, a new heart, put a new spirit in us': a new spirit, truly new and not painted over, pieced together, patched. The illustration of all this scrap metal which becomes pieces of shining new steel is a telling one.

Human beings are truly capable of involving themselves in a most profound act of repentance which renews them from top to bottom. True repentance is a rebirth.

We emerge from repentance like a baby coming out of the bath, like a child with clean fresh skin, because we have gone so deep down to the heart of our fault and touched on the depths of our misery, guilt and responsibility. Often our confessions do not renew anything in us, beause they do not get to the level of true repentance. We come out of them as we went in, and absolution slides off us like water off a duck's back. For absolution is certainly not enough in itself; in confession, what counts is not so much absolution as the depth of repentance that one feels.

A thousand years before Christ, David cried out his fault, and expressed his misery in lament; he tore his clothes, he rent his heart, and from this emerged his feelings expressed in Psalm 51 – an eternal, unforgettable, immortal psalm:

> Have mercy upon me, O God, after your great goodness:
> according to the multitude of your mercies do away my offences.
> Wash me thoroughly from my wickedness:
> and cleanse me from my sin.
>
> For I acknowledge my faults:
> and my sin is ever before me.

The grace of God is commensurate to the abyss which repentance opens up in us. What we lack is the sense of our guilt, the sense of our sin – a sense, however, which is not despair or vain remorse, but true repentance.

We have to go to the roots of our being to rediscover the source. In repentance there is a secret of youth, a secret of life, a secret of extraordinary childlikeness. We usually live in the middle zones of our being. We half-sin and we half-repent. We half-look at our sin and we half-turn to God. Everything about us is half-hearted, and takes place in the intermediate areas of a frightful mediocrity. We are neither dead nor alive, nor hot nor cold, but lukewarm. So our repentance is not true repentance, but a formality – or worse, self-justification. We tell ourselves, 'In the end it's not as bad as all that – everyone does it.' We plead all kinds of mitigating circumstances. We dress up our sin in the best clothes, we decorate it, disguise it, and bring it to the Lord in the form of a very little fault, quite gentle, cute, touching. At heart we have already given ourselves absolution and feel justified. This refusal to take responsiblity for our faults is connected with the fact that we have no other alternatives than remorse and despair. For us, culpability takes on only one face – that of the bad conscience, the scruple, and this 'morbid universe of sin' evoked at every moment. It is because we are imprisoned in this false sense of guilt that we reject it.

But what I want to bring out is the other face of guilt, that of repentance. Repentance is not afraid to get down to the heart of a fault, to the depths of being. In true guilt I take my fault in my hands, I look it in the face, I recognize it, I accept it, I take responsibility for it while at the same time repudiating it.

Our ultimate dignity and greatness as human beings lies in the way in which we take responsibility for our actions. Human beings know that they are responsible, want to be responsible. When we seek to veil our guilt and deck it out with all kinds of more or less specious motives, with more or less imaginary justifications, we refuse this responsibility.

A while ago someone said to me in confession, 'Father, I have committed a very serious sin. I did so not by mistake but freely, deliberately and willingly. I accuse myself of it and I regret it from the bottom of my heart.' As I listened to this confession I bowed my head and said to myself, 'That's beautiful...'

Acute awareness of our faults and true repentance is what helps us to get to the bottom of things, makes us reach the source, and renews us.

To refuse to accept guilt is to refuse to progress and move beyond oneself. When guilt gets to the heart of being, it causes a rebound, like a ball falling to the ground. When it reaches the ground and makes contact with it, it bounces back. Human beings are not often capable of rebounding, because they do not want to touch the ground of their being, because they refuse to fall to their depths. So there is no reprise, no renewal, no going beyond.

As Jean Lacroix commented,

The true feeling of guilt arises out of a self-criticism which is the recognition of a deficiency, an incompleteness, and at the same time an awareness of the effort by which we can pursue our achievement.

So repentance involves recognizing a deficiency. How can one remedy this deficiency without first recognizing it? The self-examination of which I spoke earlier is precisely this recognition of a deficiency, and once that has been done, the deficiency can be compensated for and made good. But if there is no awareness, no self-criticism, we can no longer rise above ourselves and we are stuck in our mediocrity.

A refusal to recognize that one is a sinner is one of the most frequent causes of a state of lukewarmness and essential mediocrity.

How was it possible for the robber crucified alongside Jesus to be able to wipe out a whole life of crime by his one act of repentance? Jesus promised him: 'Truly, I say to you, today you will be with me in paradise!' (Luke 23.43).

It is precisely because this man penetrated so deeply into himself that in this sole act of repentance he was capable of renewing his whole life, of ransoming all his past. We may protest at this forgiveness granted freely and immediately by Christ, and say, 'But that's unfair.' Christ replies to us, 'No, it's fair.' For though this man may not be capable of obliterating all the evil actions he has done and all the crimes that he has committed, in his profound intention and his essential being he is capable of wishing himself otherwise, of choosing afresh to give his life a new dimenison. That is what conversion is. It is choosing oneself anew and wanting oneself anew. And that is also hope.

The good news given to us is that everything can be taken up again, everything can be begun again, everything can be redeemed, everything can be recreated.

This return to the source of our being, to the source of things, is conversion. Conversion is a return to the first morning of the world when the light shone from the darkness. Moreover, the word conversion (*convertere*) means resuming, turning round. I take up my life and turn it inside out, as one may turn a bag inside out. I make something new out of the old.

A young man condemned to death said before he died, 'I am worth more than my life.'

This amazing remark indicates that this young man, who had committed all kinds of crimes and atrocities, was aware at the moment of his death that they did not express his true life, his true self. In strictly legal terms he was guilty. But in the depths of his heart, he told himself, 'All that is not me.' Which of us, after a sinful action, has not felt deep within ourselves that what we have done is not us? True repentance does not consist in denying that we have done evil, but in standing above it and telling ourselves, 'Yes, that's fair, I've done wrong, but the wrong that I have done wrong is not the deepest expression of my life. I refuse to identify myself with it.' 'I am worth more than my fault.' I wanted it and at the same time I did not want it, as Paul was aware (Romans 7).

In other words, I repudiate my past, not by refusing to take responsibility for it, but by saying, 'I am worth more than my past: I do not want to be what I have been.' Conversion is a return to my original self, to the person at the roots. Conversion is going beyond the law.

If we wanted to make another comparison between remorse and repentance, we might say that remorse is at the level of the law, while repentance is at the level of grace. The law is fixed and firm: 'Did you do this?' 'Yes.' 'You will be condemned.' 'That's fair, I deserved it.'

There was transgression, so there will be judgment; that is penal guilt.

Repentance is another matter. Repentance is not on the same level as penal justice but is at the level of moral justice. It is not at the level of penal culpability but at that of moral culpability, and that is quite different: it is grace, it is conversion, it is rebirth.

Now while we are imprisoned in the law, while we are imprisoned in the Ten Commandments, while we are imprisoned in a kind of moralizing morality, we can only be encouraged in a feeling of morbid guilt and remorse. The majority of men and women are still in that state.

But let us look again at St Paul, at his letters to the Romans and to the Galatians: 'You are no longer under the law, but under grace' (Rom.6.14). The law is condemnation. The law is morbid guilt. The law is sterile remorse. The law is the past in which one is shut up and to which one is chained. But, grace is the future; grace is hope; grace is rebirth; grace is the remission of sins.

When Jesus is asked, 'Are you the one who is to come or do we look for another?' (Luke 7.19), he replies: 'Go and announce that the blind see, the deaf hear, the lame walk, the lepers are cured and the dead raised' (Luke 7.22).

What does that mean? It means that with Christ there is a new creation, a total remaking of this world.

All these cures and resurrections on a physical level are simply the sign of another cure, another resurrection, on the level of essential being, on the level of sin and grace. That is what Christ meant when he cured the paralysed man: 'Is it easier to say "Your sins are forgiven" or "Take up your bed and walk"?'

The forgiveness of Jesus is the very act which remakes a person, renewing him or her at the centre. Our forgiveness, too, is an act which can recreate others and renew them at the centre. It consists in saying to the other person, 'Your past is forgotten, rubbed out. I'm giving you a chance; you can begin your life again.' To this desperate, crushed, humiliated person I am offering the possibility of a ransom, the possibility of redemption.

In a school there are always bad pupils, trouble-makers. The danger is that these children will be classified as belonging to that category and in effect be told, 'Nothing can be done with you. It will never be possible to do anything with you. You're a failure.' Once this has been said, the child will always remain a failure. We have fixed the child in his or her past without offering any chance of a fresh start. This child is lost, cursed, condemned for ever, shut up in its past.

Husband and wife, or friends, will often remind each other of past faults: 'Remember, you did that to me, you said that to me. You did the same thing again last year, last month.' 'Yes, I remember, that's right. So I did.' You hang your head while the other person attacks you even more, tramples on you even harder, vilifies you even worse, enjoying the revenge. Then you say, 'Yes, that's right, I did that, but what about you? You did that to me; you said that to me.' This quarrel is war, the vicious circle of morbid guilt.

Forgiveness consists in saying to the other person, 'I know that you did all that, but you did it in spite of yourself; you weren't the one who was doing it; someone else was doing it in you. Basically you didn't want to do it. Everything is forgotten, blotted out, forgiven.' And at that moment there is the possibility of ransom, the hope of redemption.

That reminds me of a little incident which happened when I was teaching at a preparatory school. One of my pupils, who had had polio, full of complexes and crushed by a terrible feeling of inferiority, had become tough and aggressive with his friends. He pinched, pulled, hit, insulted them, watching them enviously as they played football or rushed around, while he remained in his corner, condemned to immobility by his infirmity. That had made him naughty and he avenged himself for it. One day I called him and said to him. 'You're being naughty like this despite yourself. Basically you've a heart of gold. Deep down you're good, very good.' The child then burst into tears in my arms and cried as though he couldn't stop. Beyond all his hateful behaviour he felt that someone understood that he was basically good, that his soul was overflowing with tenderness and affection. And from that day on he made progress; he was transformed and became sweet, gentle, smiling, affectionate, because I had been able to show him his other face.

That is what Christian forgiveness is: drawing a veil over the past, beginning on a new page, giving the other person a chance and allowing him or her to begin afresh.

The gospel says to us, 'Do not judge' (Matt.7.1).

Yes, do not judge, do not condemn, for you do not know what is hidden in a person. What you know and what you judge is the past, but you do not know the future, and the past is full of promise. I've known desperate people who have said to me: 'I'm ruined, there's nothing I can do, I've spoilt my life.' But given an attitude of patience, attention and hope on our part, such people can change, can be radically changed, profoundly changed, and become new creatures.

To act in this way is to open up a gateway of hope, to offer redemption. We are responsible for one another, and by a certain faith, a certain attitude, we can recreate and raise up those who come to us, those around us. Redemption is possible: the redemption of time, the redemption of the past, the redemption of faults.

If we are truly to arrive at this level of forgiveness we have to begin by recognizing that we ourselves are sinners and are ourselves in need of forgiveness. It is often because we cannot recognize our own faults that we cannot excuse the faults in others. In the Our Father we say, 'Forgive us our trespasses, as we forgive them that trespass against us.' It is in recognizing our own sin that we become capable of pardoning the sin of others and bringing about reconciliation.

Jean Lacroix has expressed his vision of a new sacrament, the sacrament of the future, conjugal confession:

Conjugal confession is the essence of marriage, because love consists in constantly giving the other a chance to start again. Love is continual creation and recreation.

That is why the Dane Kierkegaard says that basically, at the very heart of guiltiness, there is forgetting. His God, like the God of the Bible and the gospel, is a God who forgets. There is no true love without forgetting.

This is not a forgetting caused by old age or infirmity, but a deliberate, agreed forgetting. We often carry around in the depths of our hearts grievances which go back to childhood, to adolescence, to the beginning of our marriage or some such period of our life. We have made a list of other people's mistakes that we never stop mulling over. But forget, forget! The other person has changed, is no longer the same, and is basically better than we think. He or she must be given a chance, be healed and reborn. We should not keep harping on the past; we should turn the page, and then we shall see a new being in front of us. To know how to forget is one of the supreme virtues.

There is no true love without forgetting. That is what forgiveness is.

Let us look at the way in which Jesus regards sinners. This is not the Sartrean look of God which fixes, judges and condemns, but the look of hope which gives courage, and confidence. Jesus looks at the woman of Samaria and says, 'You have had five men and the one you have at present is not your husband' (John 4.17-18). He looks at her, and yet she does not feel either judged or condemned. And Mary Magdalene, the sinner, the courtesan, the public woman, sits at Jesus' feet while he looks right into her heart. She too is not obliterated by this gaze, but she cries tears of repentance, and her heart is transformed.

And the adulterous woman: 'Woman, I do not condemn you.' Her accusers are there, full of hatred: 'She has sinned.' 'Yes, she has sinned.' 'She has committed adultery.' 'Yes, she has commited adultery.' 'She must be stoned.' But Jesus answers: 'Let him among you who is without sin cast the first stone' (hypocrites!) (John 8.7-11).

We are all hypocrites, because we excel at accusing one another in our well-educated society, and as we sit and talk, calumny is often distilled like a poison. Let the one who is without sin cast the first stone at this fallen woman, at this man who has gone wrong, at this other person how has dirtied his hands. You who find fault with the dirt of others, are you aware of all the rottenness deep within yourself? It is in recognizing your own sin and guilt that forgiveness will become possible for you.

The look that Jesus gave to Judas and to Peter was the same look that he gave to the woman of Samaria, to Mary Magdalene, to the woman taken in adultery. Judas did not understand, but Peter did, and it was this look which broke his heart and called forth a torrent of tears.

The look which Jesus directs towards us is a look of compassion, a look of redemption, a look of ransom, a look of resurrection, a look of hope. And as Fr Baudiquey said in a famous poem, 'The only glances of love are those which make us hope.' Only the look that is capable of discerning the new person behind the lowest, most vilified, the most ravaged being, waiting for rebirth and resurrection, is a creative look, a look of redemption, a look of hope.

That is the redemption of time.

But this look and this redemption are possible only when my sin is a sin not confronting me, but the one who can save me.

I quoted earlier a phrase from Psalm 51, 'My sin is ever before me.' My sin can be ever before me like a foul and morbid obsession, but it can also project me forward towards the one who can rid me of it, tear me away from it. That is why the psalm also adds, 'Against you only have I sinned.'

Those who sin before God do not sin against themselves, do not debate with themselves in a sterile and exhausting fight, but place themselves before the one who alone is capable of extricating them from sin.

Nothing is finished, nothing is lost, nothing is to be regretted. All is grace, all can be saved, all can be redeemed. The blind see, the deaf hear, the lame walk, the lepers are healed, the dead are raised. Through all these signs, God tells us: 'I who can cure the body and recreate it can also cure your soul and recreate it. Little person, I can remake you, create you anew. The ultimate sign of the kingdom is the resurrection. And the resurrection is a new person, a new heart, a new spirit, a new being.

The resurrection does not consist in rediscovering a body doomed again to death. I am not interested in living another life which will end in a new death, in that eternal beginning-again of successive resurrections and indefinite reincarnations. No, I dare to hope for something else, something different from this life which keeps getting longer and longer and which doctors promise us will develop until one day soon we shall live to be a hundred, a hundred and twenty, a hundred and fifty. No thank you, Lord! I dare to hope for something other than this indefinitely prolonged old age, going on and on, or the slow death which never seems to come.

What I want is eternal life, life which does not die, life with a capital L, which is continual rebirth, perpetual flow. What I want is a body which does not decay, a body which does not perish, a resurrection body. That is our hope, when the Lord takes our flesh and bones to make us new, like the scrap iron which the furnace transforms into new and shining steel.

This was the hope which the French poet Charles Péguy celebrated in a famous hymn. In his enormous verse epic *Eve*, almost two thousand strophes long, depicting the salvation history of humankind, in a vision he depicts the coming into being of another, new, world involving the material of the old and the resurrection of the dead.

This new world will contain our past reshaped, fused in the glowing love of a future which will never fade, which can never be extinguished, since we shall be eternal, and there will be no more death.

In a providential way, the text of the mass for the day on which I am finishing this chapter coincides with the idea that I have just been developing. So let me take these words from the Revelation of John as a sign for us and as the end of this chapter:

I saw a new heaven and a new earth, for the first heaven and the first earth had passed away (Rev.21.1).

We shall no longer remember the past and our life on earth, happy, but also full of mistakes; it will no longer come back to us on that level, but we shall delight in the joy and eternal happiness of what God is to create. There we shall not see but *taste* with happy hearts and in ardent joy the transformation and consummation of our life rediscovered for us by the divine hand.

On many occasions priests accumulate the concerns of desperate people in their prayers. So I have summed them all up in a prayer to focus our meditation on feelings of guilt and redemption:

To the Master of the Universe

Lord, your sovereign power conquered nothingness
when you brought the universe into being.
Help me to believe
in your infinite power,
which creates each day in a new realm.

Lord, your spirit went over the primal waters of creation
to make them fertile.
Help me to believe

in the lifegiving power of this spirit,
present in my heart and in the heart of the world.

Lord, you conquered the darkness
and made the primal light shine at your bidding.
Help me to believe
that your word will make a sun rise
from the depths of my night.

Lord, the gleam of your light breaks through all nights
in its fullness, its clear shining.
Tear off all the veils in me
and make it day,
your day in me.

Lord, you willed and created teeming life
and enabled it to inhabit the material earth.
Help me to believe in this wonder,
because it will conquer death and decay.

Lord, you made trees and woods grow,
buds spring up and flowers bloom.
Help me to believe
in this eternally new mystery
in its never wearying power, because it is you yourself.

Lord, you ordered chaos, by forming in your hands
a universe in beauty and harmony.
Help me to believe
that you can correct our errors
and can change our uglinesses into masterpieces of grace.

Lord, at the beginning of time you bent over us
and lovingly steeped us in your spirit.
Help me to believe that you will not stop
bending over our guilt
so that we can be born eternally new in you.

Lord, you have created me in your image
and according to your likeness.
Create anew once again
the countenance that I lost,
and make it like yours.

Lord, you have called me your son,
your only son.
Help me to believe inwardly
in this fatherly heritage
and surrender myself to your motherly arms.

Lord, you tested Abraham but did not forsake him
when he went through this night.
Help me never to doubt
in your presence,
and preserve me victorious in my faith.

Lord, you snatched your people from slavery
and freed them from pressure and servitude.
Help me also to become free
from all that chains me, fetters me, binds me.

Lord, you made a firm way for your people
through the depths of the sea.
For me, too, in the sea of my sorrow
open up a way to salvation.

Lord, you went with your people
through wilderness and solitude.
Help me always to feel your presence,
when every support and all help fails.

Lord, you will prepare for your people
a land where milk and honey flow.
Help me to believe
in this kingdom of gentleness and love,
your promise at the end of our way.

Lord, you have made the blind see
and the deaf hear.
Open my eyes, too, to your light,
and my ears to your truth.

Lord, you healed the sick
and lepers became clean.
Heal and purify me also
from my weaknesses, suffering and infirmities.

Lord, you forgave the adulteress
and freely accepted the sinner.

Accept me also in your understanding heart
and save me by the power of your love.

Lord, you opened your arms to the prodigal son
and took him to your heart.
Accept me also in my poverty,
and have mercy on me in the grief of my failure.

Lord, you bade the storm be still
above the turbulent waters, and calmed them.
Smoothe the waves in my sorrowing soul
and give them your peace.

Lord, you strode safely over the waters
despite the challenge of the elements.
Deliver me from the power of evil,
and rescue me from its undertow.

Lord, you enabled Peter
to do as you did on the surface of the water.
Help me, too, to conquer doubt which holds danger
and anxiety which paralyses me.

Lord, you resisted temptation,
strengthened by fasting, fortified by prayer.
Help me also to withstand my test
by rooting myself still more firmly in you.

Lord, you drove out demons
and rescued people from their attack.
Preserve me also from negative influences
and alienation from myself.

Lord, you fettered and cast out
the prince of this world.
Help me to feel your powers within me
and remove me from the sphere of evil.

Lord, you said, 'Behold, I make all things new.
These words are true and faithful.'
Make me today a new heart
and fill me with new spirit.

Lord, it is written,
'Behold the tabernacle of God is with men.

He will dwell among them.
He will wipe all tears from their eyes
and death will be no more,
nor sorrow nor lamentation nor tribulation,
the former things are past.'
Help this tremendous hope to gain strength within me
when suffering seeks to suffocate me
and death embraces me.

Lord, you have said,
'He who believes in me will live,
even though he is dead.'
Help me to believe inwardly in your life,
your final victory and your triumph,
over all that is evil.

Lord, you have said,
'I am the resurrection and the life.'
Help me now and every day to rise in you
in order to live from you – wholly from you.

7   All is Grace

'Do not fear evil, for it may bring you good'
(*Arabic saying*)

All is grace. From the very beginning of cosmic existence all is
grace, since creation is a free gift. Creation is grace, the first of all
graces – a gift of God.

'But sin came into the world, and with sin, death' (Romans
5.12). Evil manifested itself in space and time, entered history and
took part in it. The gracious gift of creation became stained. Evil
grew, multiplied, raged, and culminated in the greatest of all
human sins, which is called the 'cross', or Golgotha.

'But where sin increased, grace abounded all the more' (Romans
5.20b). Thanks to this cross, this crucified man on the cross,
universal redemption took place and our fallen world was established anew. The free gift of creation was followed by the free gift
of redemption. Since then, countless members of a new human
race have looked towards a different goal of creation, 'a new
heaven and a new earth' (cf. Rev.21.1).

This new humanity took its beginning in the days of the death
and resurrection of Jesus. The moment of its birth was the time
when a promise recorded in the book of Isaiah was fulfilled,
'Behold, I make all things new' (43.19).

The redemption of Golgotha is this new creation, and in
particular it is a new creation of humankind. This process is taking
place as a result of the workings of grace, through which the
whole of creation since the moment of the dawning of light up to
the complete transformation and consummation of the history of
this universe is taken up into the divine stream of grace. We
recognize the free gift of God as a source at the centre, flowing
out in two directions: back to the origin of all things and forward
to the new goal of creation. This source of grace sprang from the

hill of Golgotha, as it had sprung from the rock in the burning wilderness when Moses touched it.

It is interesting to read in the legend of creation that God begins with the creation of heaven, earth and light. Then God brings into being plants bearing seed and fruit trees, and sets 'lights in the firmament'. What a glorious fresco is painted here!

After that, 'swarms of living creatures' are said to have been created in the sea; then God created fowls, wild animals and cattle, and finally, right at the end, human beings, who were to inaugurate a new era. They are completely different...

By contrast, the New Testament begins with the last member of this human race, again opening a new era. Now, through him, the new Adam, a people of God slowly begins to develop and to strive towards a goal of development through history, that 'new heaven above a new earth'. One has the impression that here something is incrasingly narrowing and becoming concentrated on itself, so that it comes to a focal point in the midst of this tremendous history. From there it develops outwards and extends further, to become a multitude of 144,000 people – a symbolic number which means 'tremendously great'. The focal point through which history runs is called Jesus Christ. When the new heaven appears over a new earth, we recognize the significance, the goal and the end of this grandiose saving event which began with the redemptive death of Jesus Christ.

At the heart of this movement in history we find the mystery of this death, but we know that this mystery is at the same time a mystery of resurretion. The two are identical, since they mean resurrection in death and resurrection for death. 'Death has been destroyed by death,' sing believers in the Byzantine Easter liturgy. 'Death has trampled on death and opened up the way for those who rest in the grave.' This powerful impetus, this brilliant dawning of a completely new life, born out of the mysterious depths of this crucifixion, is the paradox and apparently insurmountable contradiction in our Christian mystery. Death means life and life means death.

Deep within this death there is a fertile field in which human salvation takes root and puts down shoots. From this miraculous earth, eternal life now grows up in all its strength. It germinates and grows out of death, presses towards development, and will blossom for us all. Golgotha, a crucified man, an opened side from which the source of grace sprang, to permeate and heal the world! The fruit of redemptive death is grace.

What is grace? Grace is the life of God's own self. Grace means life, but far more than the ordinary life that we know. We know that the ordinary life of Adam most certainly leads to death. His life bears him there, just as the whole of the first creation falls victim to death. But there is already a second creation which we call the history of redemption, and this leads beyond death to another goal: it leads to eternal life. It leads to eternal life because it now has its source in the new Adam, in the divinized human being who bears this lifespring in himself. So the mystery of grace means boundless light, hope, deep confidence, for eternal life means life in God.

What does grace mean in everyday life? We find almost the same word in many languages and with the same meaning: *gratia, gratis, gratuit,* and so on; it always means 'free gift', a present. In our human society, a world of trade and business, everything costs something; it all has a price that has to be paid. But at the same time we also form a human community of the children of God in which we receive freely, *gratis*. In and with God we live *'en famille'*. Are there any families in which payment is expected before anyone can have anything to eat? No, one may take without payment or hesitation, quite naturally, since at home everything is gratis.

God's offer is of the same kind, for our relationship to this offer is that of being children of God, and our life in the community of the world is *en famille*. Everything is free. Unfortunately modern men and women have lost the sense of this free approach of and to God, since they are utterly dominated by the commercial thinking of a world of painfully accurate calculation and correct bookkeeping. Our conception of a life with God, a spiritual life, has become distorted, as have our human personal relationships. How rare is the kind of relationship which is so free and authentic that everything is free on both sides!

In a European country I saw a young girl visiting her mother and eating lunch with her. Before she went, she paid her mother for the meal. But there is no need to resort to such extreme cases to be aware that our mode of existence is basically a calculating one. Our life is one long transaction: I give you this – you give me that. I gave you a splendid present, so you should have given me one in return. Since I'm still waiting, don't expect any more of me... These are really impossible conversations, and yet they happen so frequently in the quiet secrecy of a speculating heart. But a gift which is not a completely free offering to someone else ceases to be a gift. The good relationship between two human beings can no longer be called 'good', since often the cost of a gift is carefully worked out and compared, and woe to anyone who has bought and given below the other's price level!

By calculating, we allow deep shadows to fall upon our human relationships, which prevent them from growing. Gently but clearly, ugly tensions become evident, and the pressure of this reciprocal having-to-give dominates; it is almost impossible to find that bright sphere of pure joy which goes with a real present. I know what I am saying, because I myself belong to this bourgeois society in which people put one another under pressure with their gifts. I am delighted only by truly free presents, when I know that there is no hidden calculation behind them, for I long so much for another world, a world of mutually free gift.

Among free gifts I also include all contributions towards mutual help and service, spontaneous self-giving without expecting anything in return. That already begins in schools where brave teachers work year in and year out with difficult pupils, never getting anything back in recompense. Let us take that as the best example, and all work in this attitude of sheer giving. Let us become sons of the one 'who makes his sun rise on the evil and the good, and who sends rain on the just and on the unjust' (Matthew 5.45).

The one of whom we are thinking here is the one who certainly does not look for anything in return. I was always an opponent of the so-called spiritual payment of God through litanies. I simply cannot believe that God wants to be paid, either after a gift of grace or before it, by being begged for it. I have always been saddened when watching people trying to do business with God. For great graces a novena or a triduum, for smaller favours of heaven less would suffice – perhaps a rosary. As if there were a heavenly tariff which we human beings could set!

This is a lapse into the trade in indulgences from olden days. I had a dear old aunt who spent her time sitting in a pew with her rosary. She ardently sought to liberate this or that soul from purgatory and incessantly paid the tariff in the form of countless prayers and appeals. That was her religious mentality, and she acted with the best intentions, so I won't criticize her here. But that sort of thing led to excesses in our churches which make your hair stand on end, and one feels sympathy for the Protestants who at one point reacted so strongly against the system of trafficking in indulgences, especially as unfortunately it had also developed into a thriving business. No, God really does not need to be paid by us, nor does he want to. How could God be bought? All is grace.

People also seek to secure divine favour with works; they try to redeem themselves or keep in God's good books by what they do. This commercial way of thinking is very widespread, and extends right into our modern spiritual communities. Certain of good will and with the utmost generosity, with growing zeal people offer God more and more hours of work and promise to spend them in pious service for him. An eight-hour day becomes a twelve-hour day; soon it gets up to fourteen and attempts are made to make it sixteen. 'I will sleep less and work more, eat less and pray more. Lord, you must be pleased with me!' But we must listen carefully to the words of Jesus when he was the guest of two very different sisters: 'Martha, Martha, you are anxious and troubled about many things; one thing is needful. Mary has chosen the good portion, which shall not be taken away from her' (Luke 10.41f.).

The time comes when God speaks to the overzealous, for when they do too much of his work, it destroys their inner peace: 'That's enough! Stop! Break off! Relax and find rest with me. Smile, let yourself go for a while and feel that I love you. I love you. Can't you feel it? I love you. Can't you accept it?'

The true Christian attitude does not consist primarily in loving so much as in knowing and accepting the love of God. Let's look at that more closely. It is always much simpler to give than to receive. We don't understand that properly. In the zeal of our faith we grit our teeth and go on working, but letting go and surrendering to God is also an attitude of faith, since it is evidence of trust; indeed it is already prayer. At that moment people cease to give and only receive, in other words, contemplate God with their whole soul and listen to his word, as Martha's sister Mary did.

Human beings should not degrade themselves to the point of becoming machines, but they should be receptive souls. God does not want us to kill ourselves with work; that is certainly not his will. He did not create us to kill ourselves in that way; in everything that we have to do we need to be able to be quite relaxed, to pray with a smile and to keep silent – the signs of deepest spiritual relaxation. Then our being can adjust itself to the being of God. But think of all the misunderstandings there can be here. People rush through a series of prayers because they only have fifteen minutes to spare, and at the end they have frustrated God by not letting him get a word in edgeways. A prayer is not a monologue but a dialogue, a dialogue of love. Let us be sensitive to our creator and feel his call: 'Be silent and listen. Rest and let me be active now!'

This experience of emptiness and radical poverty bears witness to the deepest attitude that we can adopt before God. At this moment we share in an experience of grace. Without any visible reason, without any previous effort, quite contrary to our expectations, we are given a gift, a pure gift. 'If only you knew the gift of God...'(John 4.10).

That saying comes from the episode in St John's Gospel in which Jesus drinks from Jacob's well. He is speaking of grace. Just as the Samaritan woman gives Jesus water here, so we human beings give God water in the form of human friendship, human work, human love. He even asks for it and accepts it gratefully. But the moment comes when he wants us to be on the receiving end, when he wants to give us something, to give quite different water: the water of eternal life as a free gift to us. This is the experience of the grace of God.

Prayer, too, is ultimately a gift to us, a gift of God, so it is better to go to prayer with empty hands. For if our hands are full of good works which we joyfully offer up to God, there is no room for God to put anything in them. At times we have to be able to set everything aside and forget it: all our duties and tasks, all our own plans, in order to be able to go to God completely naked, simply to receive. Then the Lord will surprise us, astound us, shake us, for he will fill our hands to overflowing. We shall receive treasure beyond our dreams. But in prayer one first has to have the experience of radical poverty.

Here I would like to distinguish between faith and love for God. We are accustomed to hearing that our love stands right at the top of the table of values, for in his great hymn of praise in I Corinthians 13 Paul writes that of faith, love and hope, love is the greatest.

From this text people have inferred that the love of neighbour is our most noble impulse and our most noble action. I may indeed attempt that. I may work hard to love God and others as much as I can; but I know that there is another attitude, which consists in letting oneself be loved. Perhaps this attitude is the greater and more important one; as John tells us in his first letter, love is not that we loved God but that God loved us and sent his Son (I John 4.10).

Even more profound than love is faith, faith in love. Of course it is noble and praiseworthy on our part to love God, and we should certainly try to do that; but it is more, better, greater, to know that we are loved most deeply by God. For what is my mere human capacity to love compared with the immeasurable power of the divine heart? By contrast it can only be a dull glow, since it shines from a limited human heart, no matter how much that heart loves. And how often it is lukewarm or dried up, cramped or cold! If that is the case we are not to engage in psychological gymnastics in order to arouse feelings of love which warm our hearts to the love of God, but must set our being on receiving love, and allow ourselves to be warmed by it.

The experience of radical poverty of which I spoke then turns into an experience of fullness: the initial emptiness is the presupposition for the later fullness. The poorer we make ourselves, the richer our prayer. Those who have completely stripped themselves can have the experience of the over-abundance of a divine gift which grace brings about in them. It is those whose prayers are very modest and simple who experience that, for in quite natural humility they already know in advance that God will get to them first with his love, indeed that God has already got to them. They accept that God's love is infinitely greater than their small human love can ever be. They do not want to get above God's love, nor do they want to promise anything in return for the divine love. They will not promise anything either before or afterwards, since they know that they may go naked and poor before God at any time.

'Ho, everyone who thirsts, come to the waters; and he who has no money, come, buy and eat! Come, buy wine and milk with no money and without price' (Isaiah 55.1)

'This spring is free, free to refresh you,' says our heavenly Father. 'And to please me take, receive! Drink! It costs you nothing. It is my delight to give it to you.' I think that we need to recognize that clearly. In my view that is authentic Christian life, for people recognize God as the source and origin of love.

I grant that this attitude calls for a good deal of boldness in everyday practice, not to say audacity. Nevertheless, we must not balance God's possibilities against a gift of grace, but count on it right from the beginning. Let us be bold enough to have the most extraordinary wishes and to ask for the utmost grace for them. Let us be confident of being heard, not fear the magnitude of a grace but dare to ask for everything. We may have impossible wishes and count on their being fulfilled. We may go to God with our deepest longings and most urgent requests, and count on improbable promises, since they are all probable. That is Jesus' promise: 'Whatever you ask in prayer, believe that you receive it, and you will' (Mark 11.24).

That is my attitude to God. I have no time to consider and calculate all the things that I will promise to do, nor do I want to, since in any case I should have no time to keep this promise. So my hands remain empty. I have often asked God to solve a problem for me quickly because with the best will in the world I can't do it myself, and I find that it is solved spontaneously without my having to deck it out in ceremonious requests and solemn thanks.

Here is an example.

Some time ago I was back in the Sudan and urgently needed a car for the mission which we had started there in 1980. I had no money to buy one; the whole mission lives on Egyptian gifts dropping on hot Sudanese stones.

What a prayer! Lord, I need a car and as quickly as possible. Please see to it!

The next day I had an inspiration and went to a very rich Syrian Lebanese businessman in Khartoum, who owned a soap factory, an oil refinery and much more. I put my request to this stranger, told him of our group of young Egyptian volunteers who are strengthening the poor Sudanese Christians – moreover, four million animists live in the south of the country. I told him that there are only fifty priests in the largest country of the African continent; the diocese of Lome, which is as big as France and Italy put together, is looked after by a bishop and thirty-five priests. I told him how I had visited a priest whose parish was as big as the whole Nile delta and how he was one priest looking after forty-six churches and seven schools, caught up in a chain of insoluble problems. Moreover, in four years it might be too late for the Christians in the Sudan.

The man listened to me in silence, and someone else next to him nodded. Then I was asked when, how and in what currency I wanted to pay for this car and whether, as he assumed, I would get it at a much reduced price.

'No,' I said, 'I'm looking for someone to give me a car.' The two men were amazed, then they thought about it and talked together. A couple of days later I got the keys and became the owner of a Datsun which had hardly been driven.

And yet again I thought happily that it is true that one can put the most immodest requests to God. How glad I am that I had not asked God for a bicycle...

I am convinced that God wants us to ask for big things and not anxiously for trivia. For he wants human beings to think of greater things. The creator is generous; he is generosity in person, and he is pure love – and a Father! So let us delight him and put our trust in him.

In my daily work in Cairo and in my ministry as a priest, the problems pile up before my eyes, each more insoluble than the last. In addition there are the cares and needs of individuals seeking help, for first they go to their best friend, then to the doctor, then to the psychiatrist, and finally, with the problem still unsolved, come to the priest. How can a poor priest cope with such private matters, and such an infinite number of them?

There is one thing that I always do: I hand over this problem to the Lord in boundless trust and faith with a prayer for grace. And then I say good-bye to the poor person who has looked to me for help with the words, 'Go in peace. Your problem will be solved,' for I believe that. Now I have no statistics, but it seems to me that the Lord is gracious to me. Sooner or later, the person involved returns or calls me, overflowing with gratitude, for something with which I have had absolutely nothing to do. I have not achieved anything, but only believed that grace will be given to those who seek grace. All is grace.

God loves our empty hands and our hopeful, all-expectant hearts. He loves a boldness which aims high and can ask for everything. He delights in a faith which will take risks. This is how we can also slowly recognize that grace is not a flow nor a stream nor even a flood, but in its depth and breadth a boundless ocean. If you knew the grace of God – the infinite gift of God's grace! If only you knew how much God is ready to give you, is ready to give himself, if you open yourself to him! We need to know God's freedom, this generosity of the Lord of glory. If we have deep faith in his grace, then we can solve the most decisive questions of our existence in the simplest way. Faith is action. We need to repeat in our hearts, 'I believe in grace', for we are children of God and receive freely. In the house of my earthly father, everything is freely at my disposal, but in the house of my heavenly Father there is even more: I have received a share in the divine riches, a share in the fullness of God. That is unimaginable, but it is a starting point, something that we can believe. Here is a source to which we can turn.

Now that I have tried to answer the question 'What is grace?', I shall return to the redemptive work of grace, to its saving activity over the space and time of history, because it embraces and permeates everything at the same time.

If we look very deeply, we recognize that all is grace, even evil, death and sin. I have already said that the culmination of all sins in human history is the crucifixion of our Saviour. Human beings never did anything more reprehensible than that – one could almost call it original sin. There are theologians who do not locate original sin back at the origin of human history, as the guilt of the first Adam, but at a later time, the time of the second Adam. They see original sin as the act of rejecting the divine light which came to lighten the darkness but was misunderstood and rejected by it. The darkness crucified the light.

> The light has come into the world, and men loved darkness rather than light, because their deeds were evil. For everyone who does evil hates the light (John 3.19f.).

But we can leave that aside. I don't want to get into a theological discussion about it. However, one thing is clear. The most abysmal of all crimes became recognizable as a source of all salvation and all blessings. The thrust of the lance which also wounded the crucified Son of Man and Son of God at this time released a flood of grace which from then on streams into the world to reach all things: it is the source of eternal life for all. Since this hour of grief, the darkest and most terrifying thing in this world, the cross, has become an instrument of grace for our redemption and sanctification. The symbol of evil and death has become the symbol of life, of eternal life: it is the mathematical plus sign *par excellence*. What a remarkable dialectic – good and evil, salvation and disaster, grace and sin!

So if the supreme happiness can derive from the deepest misery, the richest blessing from the fatal wound of evil, then we should all lift up our hearts and have the unconditional confidence to be unshakeable optimists. Let us remind ourselves again that the greatest of all news, the really good news, is that all is grace, even death, evil and sin, for Jesus' death was a saving death which burst the bonds of evil. Through this grace of all graces *everything* has been ransomed, paid off, saved – everything. Through this death came the turning point, the dawn of the new time.

The cross has overturned the values of the world and stood history on its head. Where evil gathered and seized its supreme power, goodness shone over the night like a sun, because 'where sin increased, grace abounded all the more', as Paul told the Romans. Christ should not have had to be tortured to death at human hands, but on the other hand it could not have been otherwise. It had to happen that the supreme good sprang from the depths of evil, so that the new creation became even more wonderful and amazing than the first. The new man – created anew in Jesus Christ – towers in his true greatness above the old, for he was restored to a state of grace: his beauty will become slowly evident above the abysses in the process of history.

The old Latin liturgy of the mass conveyed this word for word. In the offertory we spoke of the creation of human beings in a wonderful way, and of how the new creation formed them even more wonderfully. It is the grace of God which here becomes active as a new process of life for men and women, which becomes powerfully effective. God not only forgives in his boundless love, but he reshapes men and women, better than before. God's will for salvation succeeds in bringing good out of evil – and if we try to imagine it, the sheer size of it takes away our breath completely. Saint-Exupéry penetrated to the heart of the matter when he said: 'The conviction that there is nothing to lament and nothing to regret is a great comfort for me.'

Here the stress lies on the word 'nothing'. We cannot in any way understand how the good could ever emerge from some kind of evil – and especially sin. But that is the challenge of faith. It is the conviction of faith that the impossible is possible because God is stronger than all the inadequacies of our world and all devilry.

Here I want to quote some fine texts from Nietzsche's Zarathustra in which Nietzsche says the same thing in his own way. He speaks of the 'foaming mixing-bowl of spice, in which all things are well compounded... the furthest to the nearest, fire to spirit and joy to sorrow and the wickedest to the kindest', and of the 'redeeming salt that makes everything mix well together in the bowl, for there is a salt that unites good and evil; and even the most evil is worthy to be a spice and a last over-foaming'.

Elsewhere he remarks, 'My brothers, it is wise that there is so much evil in the world,' or ,'Wisdom wills there to be things in the world which feel evil.' And he follows his remarks with thoughts like this:

> Did my disgust itself make me wings and strength to find new fountains?

> The transformation of values is the transformation of the creative.

> He who must be a creator always destroys...

> So the supreme evil belongs with the supreme good, but this is creative.

> Evil is man's best strength.

> 'Man must grow better and more evil' – thus do I teach.Evil is necessary for the Superman's best.

That is a harsh paradox – and yet a fantastic source of hope for our existence. Despite everything Nietzsche remained an atheist, but he recognized particular Christian truths which many Christians have not yet understood. He makes another comparison with the effects of an earthquake which buries fountains here and there but opens up new and stronger springs in other places. To put it more profoundly: earthquakes are needed to bring to light the inner powers of the mysteries. New springs burst out in the cataclysm of the old.

Christian optimism is Easter optimism. Christian optimists do not assert in naive tones that all will go well, but they believe in holy earnestness that even if something ends unhappily or tragically, this negative will be transformed into a positive in an unfathomable divine way. When everything goes smoothly it is easy to be an optimist; at that time no one deserves to be called an optimist. Our Christian optimism is paschal: that is, it is no easy fair-weather optimism, but a resurrection optimism which has gone through storm and hail and has survived death. It is an optimism beyond night and mist, beyond evil and death, and beyond time – an optimism which has an even stronger name, confidence.

The great among us have grasped this mystery. We heard Saint-Exupéry and Nietzsche. There are also the comments of the great German Protestant theologian Dietrich Bonhoeffer, who was executed a few weeks before the end of the Second World War after two years in Berlin prisons: 'Over the heads of the men who make history the ruler of history continually brings good out of evil... I believe that God can and will bring good out of everything, even the worst.'

That is very clearly seen and said. Evil will turn to good. But that is continuous creation, uninterrupted new creation through a change for the better. God has not only made being arise out of nothingness, but he also works incessantly at it, at this human world with all its follies and weaknesses, and at its deepest sins – starting from human sin. That is God's work of redemption and Christ's message of redemption.

Our wanderings and our errors... We all experience a fiasco at some time in our life; there is no biography without this experience of shipwreck. At that point a person may either describe the failure as catastrophe and perhaps even give up, or understand it as a blessing and a starting point for all that is essential. Words spoken which it would have been better not to utter, actions which would have been better left undone, all that we lament, that burdens us, causes disquiet, anxiety or bitterness, has been put before God in quite a new way and can be to our gain. Catastrophes are then no longer catastrophes, mistakes are no longer mistakes – so long as we believe that the creator is capable of changing everything, even evil and falsehood, into what is good and right.

I imagine that it is infinitely easier for the creator God to make his creation shine forth out of nothingness and bring a perfect world into being than incessantly to take up, change and recreate our failure towards him and creation. God forms and shapes, collects and builds up, but human beings tear down, scatter, alienate and destroy. And then God picks up what has been destroyed and reshapes it in his hands, creates it anew in a thousand ways. No matter how much human beings also damage and degrade creation, and even threaten to lose themselves in the process, they never fall out of God's hand, and in God's hand they do not remain in this state. We should certainly not believe that redemption is that unique historical act two thousand years ago in this corner of Palestine. We should speak, rather, of the redeeming event, since it continues over the course of time. Redemption is a continuous action of God in our present.

And there is our baptism. This short moment in our early life, too, does not mean our once-for-all ransom from the fangs of evil; rather, God baptizes us uninterruptedly, so that we are constantly released newborn from his creative hand. That is redemption beyond our measure of time, and not an event fixed in space and time and thus a purely historical action. Redemption is the ongoing process of recasting the world and thus above all of reshaping men and women – God's constant re-creation. God takes us and immerses us in the water of baptism, floods us with this source of renewing grace. Grace is effective in the present, at all moments. We should not say that we have received grace, but we should get used to saying that we receive graces, now, for they are at work in the depths of our being.

We also find this sign of divine alchemy, of creating good out of human powerlessness and filth as the alchemist creates gold from the meanest elements by the transmutation of metal, throughout nature, and very near to us in our own gardens. Roses spread their fragrance and blossom over the decay of a family household when this has turned to corruption and been transformed into good earth. Divine alchemy – what else? We should seek these signs, and wonder with reverence at the most remarkable metamorphoses in the sphere of nature; we should let it be an indication of redemption, for redemption is a metamorphosis of this world.

All is grace: the historical process of the church is also grace, since the deaths of its martyrs are grace. As the church lives and matures and constantly reshapes itself, it certainly does not do so, as some might assume, on the basis of the intellectual capacity of competent theologians; these merely contribute to it. Nor does it do so on the basis of its financial resources, since such success cannot be bought. No, we find the mystery of its growth in the phenomenon of weakness and death, martyr death, ongoing martyr death in the past and the present, through time and history.

Three hundred years of the persecution of Christians at the beginning of our church history is a long time, full of tragedies. The first Christians hung, like the Saviour himself, on crosses and gallows, were reviled naked in the circus or thrown to the wild beasts, were publicly flogged, tortured in prison, put on the wheel in the market place, quartered or dragged to their deaths; they were hurled into boiling oil or burnt alive. But again we observe the mystery of death and life: this fearful field of dying was a fertile field of life in which the true church grew and gained stength. Down to the present day it has its roots in this sacrificial field, in the blood of the martyrs, from which it drew its first living power and could become firm, secure and strong. Therefore it also became a sacred custom to put the relic of a martyr within the altars of the world, for the sacrament of Christ is very closely connected with the sacrament of human beings; the sacrifice of Christ is very closely connected with the sacrifice of human beings. The source of the church's life eternally remains 'three hundred years of the persecution, suffering and death of Christians'.

Consequently, the founder of our Jesuit order showed himself to be deeply concerned when the missionaries who were sent out suffered no persecution, but he received the good news that things were going well with them under emperor X in land Y, or particularly well under marchioness Z...

No, they really lacked nothing. They were given splendid villas which even the king visited. Doesn't that say it all? And the financial resources for the building up of missions flourished. All this was very unwelcome news to St Ignatius, since he felt that something was wrong here. But if someone on the other hand whispered to him that his Jesuits were being arrested and tortured, then he was reassured.

'Excellent,' he would cry. 'In that case I'm certain that they are preaching the gospel without compromise, not watered down or falsified, rather than something quite different. The proof is the obstacles that the gospel comes up against and will always come up against.' So St Ignatius. Persecution is always a sign that the kingdom of God really is the kingdom of God. Without opposition and persecution there is a danger that the preaching is only about a better kingdom of this world. That has been the experience of those who have proclaimed the gospel for almost two thousand years.

And when I send my young people to the Sudan, as I say good-bye, I don't add, 'All the best.' No, I tell them that I hope it will be tough. Terrible tropical thirst and sometimes hunger and extreme exhaustion, the strain of travelling on bad roads, nerve-wracking cancellations of flights, the indifference of the Sudanese to their words, rejection, repudiation, obstacles to their mission... That is what I tell them to hope for – and such hopes are immediately fulfilled in the Sudan.

I have to say that to them, since most of them set out with a flower behind the ear and a religious song on their lips, delighted at the adventure, enthusiastic and certain of victory. But first of all they must be milled like grains of wheat, so that they can give the Sudanese spiritual nourishment and strengthen them. Unless they are caught between the millstones there, they can give no more than their own human dedication and enthusiasm, their human words. But anyone can do that; any man or woman is in a position to do good voluntarily, to give his or her best and practise love of neighbour to the full – especially at this idealistic young age. However, for the kingdom of God quite different work is needed, and the Lord purifies these souls which he sends out accordingly. For many years our Sudan mission has been experiencing in body and soul how the Lord lets it taste the grace of suffering. The unbelievable obstacles and cares have to be welcome to us. I hope that these obstacles will always accompany us; I wish for that and ask it in prayer, for only with this blessing can a mission get going, can it be given substance and importance, duration and success. Mission needs the positive effects of suffering in time. The suffering of today is the joy of tomorrow.

So, too, only a fighting church is vital and fruitful in the world, but it wilts as soon as it has settled somewhere in perfect prosperity, as soon as it is celebrated, receives recognition and honours – as soon as people flatter churchmen and give them privileges. The era of Constantine put the church in the limelight on the stage of time and removed all its problems. One new gateway after another opened up for the church – and then what happened? When the church flourished under Constantine, its decadence began.

There is nothing worse for the church than to be firmly established. There is nothing worse for a spiritual community than to be 'well provided for'. There is nothing worse than easy

134]

access to the necessary money, nothing worse than if one can say contentedly, 'All is going well'. The decadence of the religious orders always began on the day when they had grandiose monasteries with great lands and worldly regard. Then the life stopped flowing through their veins and decline began. Without struggle and tears there is no church; it has to go the thorny way of the cross. There must be obstacles; suffering is the spur. Without suffering there is no church, and without poverty no gospel.

I would also add that all the heresies and schisms and all the other errors of the church are also graces working beyond time; in other words, they work for the success of the church of the future without its always being aware of the fact or intending that result. For at all times heresies encourage progress in the inner growth of the church, and some people claim that the church only moved forward through its grossest errors: they were a stimulus towards the better. The French for a mistake is 'la gaffe', which has two meanings: 'blunder', and the 'long pole' with which one pushes a boat from the bank, stirring up a good deal of muddy water in the process. I don't think that God is particularly bothered when the church even now makes gaffes, as long as it learns from them, and here and there is prepared to take a new course. Even the mistakes of popes and bishops don't disturb me, and there are undeniably mistakes at all times which cry to heaven. Priests, too, make many mistakes, but it is precisely through these that the church grows. All is grace!

The Second Vatican Council, the place of the resurrection of our Catholic Church, would have been neither conceivable nor practicable without the Protestant Reformation and the French and Marxist revolutions. These explosions had to take place first. So in the end it is true of every contemporary phenomenon that all is grace. This insight should give us comfort and open our eyes. In that case there should be nothing more to lament, for all that we call evil particpates in the building up of the new, future people of God.

War is one of the cruellest evils of all: the earth weeps under it, and human beings should never have invented it. But paradoxically history teaches us that war gave the impetus to greater changes which brought us human beings authentic progress as well as terrible losses in all spheres. And here I am talking about progress at a very deep level; as progressive inner growth. In some cases war can work as a powerful catalyst with evil side-effects;

it drives humankind forward from within so that it takes not only timid steps towards its goal but also great leaps which save time.

My view is that, on the whole, humanity learned more in the six years of the Second World War than in all the previous six hundred years put together. Are we not all witnesses to a fantastic firework display of international discoveries and inventions in our firmament? And where were these fireworks set off? Was it not at the pinnacle of evil – in the Great War and the subsequent distress of total collapse? Under the pressure of time the human spirit had to invent a thousand instruments of evil and develop them with science and technology, so that this spirit, aroused, sharpened and trained, could soon also create instruments of good which today serve all men and women. I see that as having happened generally in international confrontations, which for all their terror and human tragedy were nevertheless encounters that, after the conflicts died down, turned into honourable mutual efforts and true human encounters.

The best example of this today is provided by the European nations. Since the end of the Second World War they have been acting – slowly to begin with, but then increasingly so – with marked courtesy and friendliness towards one another. Asia, too, is involved as a brother, and hands are stretched out over land barriers and seas. This worldwide drawing-together cannot be overlooked; we are growing out of the heartache and ruins of the Second World War into a world community. Through war we are unlearning war. And in this connection we might also think of the quite different relationship today between white and black citizens in the United States of America, and all that had to precede this new development. Evidently this is the only way in which people learn really to reach one another, to create and sustain a brotherly and sisterly world together.

The concept of peace has a variety of aspects, not all of which are necessarily always seen together. Unfortunately peace can also act as a narcotic with ultimately negative consequences for true human well-being. Deep peace makes us go to sleep, and then acts as an anaesthetic for civilization and its progress. In times of golden peace and universal prosperity, human souls atrophy to such a degree that for fifteen years people can live on the same floor of a house and not have more to say to each other than a barely audible greeting, uttered from a closed mouth. But when we hear reports of prisons, penal camps, political arrests, and so on, over and above all the cruelty of evil we also hear of people who precisely when there is no carefree peace become brothers and sisters overnight and remain so for life, bonded together in unity through their shared bitter experience of suffering. Wherever human beings have to put up with one another in extreme situations, they do not draw away from one another but their souls become welded together – while in ideal times they tend to lose themselves, become separated, avoid one another.

The suffering of poverty also has an aspect of grace which cannot be argued away. Most people have already had this experience in dealing with the poor or living for a time in poor countries. The solidarity of the poor is a light in this darkness, which the rich neither know nor suspect. How closely the poor come together in human terms! How transparent their hearts and feelings for one another become! And war, too, creates temporary poverty.

War also deepens spiritual life: a buried religious life is uncovered and begins to stir again. Not, however, as a cheap search for comfort; something much deeper is happening here. In their care, in acute anxiety and the common experience of suffering, human beings not only draw closer together physically and practise spontaneous solidarity, but also bond themselves in a still deeper dimension to become the people of God. How many conversions were there during and after the last war, known and unknown? What is the explanation for them? Is not the reason that in such times the masks fall everywhere and men and women find their true faces in the mirror? In this situation they become truthful to themselves and to their God overnight. In suffering of every kind the unworthy comedy comes to an end. Painful though the effects of war are to experience, it is also certain that they bring out the truth about men and women. The individual is purified and becomes transparent in this furnace. All is grace.

There are Lebanese today who confirm all this for me. They tell me something like this. 'Of course our civil war is sheer madness, but on the other hand this change of climate is doing Lebanon good. We were on the point of losing ourselves; pleasure was undermining all values and devouring us. There was far too much money in this country. Couldn't we understand what has happened and what is still happening as a blessing? Nowadays, amongst the ruins of Beirut, there is a rediscovery of human depths and a new understanding of existence.'

I believe such authentic reports from the Lebanon; they seem to me to be quite true. They are reflected in the great variety of spiritual movements which blossom from this suffering earth like fresh shoots. In particular the number of young people in the Lebanon who now deliberately want to confess God was never so high, and it is constantly growing. They have found the sense of a much more authentic reality, and from now on they want to commit themselves to it. All is grace, and ultimately nothing can be pulled out from the flood of history, not even if we fail to learn otherwise, not even a war, which represents the embodiment of evil, and not even death. For redemption began with a crucifixion. That stands at the heart of the 'good news'.

Now let us look into ourselves. In the quite personal sphere we sigh or shrug our shoulders and talk of our mistakes and weaknesses. How often have we been told that we should have declared war on them and exterminated them root and branch! There is no objection to this noble principle, but it cannot be realized; it remains utopian. I have only to remember the time when I was a novice in Lebanon! Systematically, week by week, month by month, we had to discard our errors, discard them one after another, like a garment. The whole of spiritual life can be understood as a war with our errors, with perfection as the aim of the battle. But a person without faults is not a person. Human beings without faults would be the most boring creatures under the sun, and God seems wisely to allow us this or that mistake so that we remain interesting to one another.

Fortunately we all have our drawbacks, and will take some of them with us to the grave. Happily we keep them all our lives, for they are facets of our basic personal being. They also have a role. Our mistakes are the other side of our virtues, the counterpart to our good properties. One can say that we have the good properties of our mistakes, and we have the mistakes of our good properties – it amounts to the same thing.

So quite a nervous person may be full to bursting with good ideas and try to put them into practice with great energy and much dynamism; a somewhat tranquil person whose sluggishness one laments may be goodness personified, with loving readiness to accept the concerns of his or her neighbour, a person who can listen and whom one trust. But in that case how do we judge nervousness and sluggishnesss? Are these good or bad properties? Are they advantages or disadvantages? Above all, how should we behave? Always in the same way: by accepting – by accepting people as they are.

We must also accept ourselves with the weaknesses which get in our way, great or small, and with the faults that we cannot get rid of. We must be able to laugh at ourselves. A sense of humour is a good help towards accepting ourselves. We need to laugh at our failings and limitations and not be afraid, for our faults are not bigger than we are. If we do that, others too will laugh with us at ourselves and our faults and like us as we are. Unfortunately the art of accepting ourselves seems to be a difficult one. However, our motto must be: 'Begin by accepting yourself, and you will be accepted; begin by loving yourself and you will be loved.'

We need above all to give up our enthusiasm for developing a faultless, unobjectionable nature: that applies most particularly to those called to the religious life or to the priesthood, since this is an illusion. We have to learn to develop along with our defects and within our limitations, and especially through them, since they may prove important equipment for us. How do we derive any advantage from our mistakes, defects and limitations? That, too, needs to be learned. To create his famous David, Michelangelo used a piece of marble which to begin with seemed to him impossible: it was too small. But instead of waiting, or looking round for a larger block, he set to work. And so his David was created within these limitations. To his genius were added these difficult circumstances, which compelled the artist to create a masterpiece. We are now convinced that there would have been no David had circumstances been easier for the master. Works of genius always arise out of a compulsion, a pressure. Here the great achievement derives from an overcoming of the obstacles. That is the thorny law of life. Obstacles and limitations make extraordinary things possible. Did you know that the great Moses and the great Jeremiah were miserable speakers (Ex.4.10-13; Jer.1.6-9)?

We have thousands of excuses to give God, so the Lord once called twelve weak and ignorant people as an example and an encouragement for us. At least ten of the apostles were very simple and uneducated men, but he called them on account of their poverty and weakness. Most significant events in world history are continually brought about by people without academic qualifications. So there is no need for us to have a complex about our intellectual background if we want to become active and make our personal contribution to society. The decisive thing is for us to have trust and to get to work. With the little that we have inherited we can work wonders and change the face of the earth. We have only to believe.

Above all, we have to accept what we were yesterday: we have to accept our past fully, along with our education, the social environment into which we were born, our health and our appearance, with all their defects and disadvantages. We must not dream of being otherwise. I know people who waste their lives burning with envy for others – and for so many reasons! Then comes a time when they become embittered or get stuck imitating people. If only they knew that they had enough good stuff in them to make a wonderful person who could have amazing success in life! But the spirit of the age dictates in us admiration for particular people who seem to us to live in splendour and glory, though when we get closer to them they are deadly boring. And there are the unknown, the insignificant, the unattractive people who captivate us precisely because of their inner being. God gave all of us many positive characteristics which make us lovable if only they can be brought to light. And we should work with this 'best part'.

However, in personal conversations I often hear nothing but the word 'if'. If I had more energy, if I had more time, if I had more money, if I had a diploma, if I could study in America, if I had contacts... This word 'if' saps people's energy and they never get started. But think of all the people whom we call great who were neither well-educated, nor in perfect health, nor so rich as to be able to carry out their plans quickly and smoothly. Many great people had very little at their disposal: only empty hands and a frail or even suffering body. But in their weakness they mobilized in the spirit the little that they had, as does everyone else, and then they believed unshakeably in their goal.

The whole secret of working wonders lies in faith. Those among us who do not believe are those who stand before us chock-full of knowledge and education but who clearly have not developed any personal life. They have no sense of even the most natural things in life, often not even of that relationship with one's neighbour which is so important. They either stand around helplessly or go off in the wrong direction. At home, framed diplomas hang on their walls, a promising future under glass, and in addition they enjoy brilliant health; some of them even have

140]

private fortunes. But nothing comes of all that! They do not desire, want or dare anything. Or they wait... They keep waiting for a still better opportunity and want circumstances to be even more favourable. They wait and demand – that is all that they 'do'. But real action would be their faith – and in faith that would be a start. Those who hesitate with their eternal excuses age very quickly: how quickly the inner person dies without plans! As Emmanuel Mounier commented, 'One should not wait until something is ripe before beginning an undertaking.' We need to begin with the little that we have been given and believe in it; if we do, then grace will be given us with which to work wonders.

Five thousand people once followed Jesus into the wilderness 'like sheep without a shepherd', including many who were sick, 'and he took pity on them and healed them'. Towards evening the twelve disciples worried about how this enormous crowd was to be fed, far from the city. When a child was brought to Jesus who had five loaves of bread and two fishes, Jesus said, 'Make the people sit down.' Then he held the child's basket, took the bread, prayed softly, and broke it and divided it, and afterwards the two fishes. At the end of the feeding of the multitude he told the apostles to go round and gather up the fragments so that nothing was left, and they came back with twelve basketsful. This is a story which is told in all four Gospels.

All is grace! We should reflect as often as possible on this miracle of the multiplication of the loaves. We need to offer the Lord the little that we have and ask him to bless it. Perhaps I, too, can feed thousands with my five loaves and two fishes, for in that case the one involved is not myself but the one who has blessed the little that I have.

Grace proves increasingly fruitful. It turns our natural gifts into supernatural, wonderful gifts. 'If only you knew the gift of God.' Those are words of Christ. If only you knew the power of grace, if only you could accept your poverty, if only you had sufficient faith! 'Believe in the power of God which is perfected in weakness' – that is the testimony that Paul left behind for us like a legacy. Paul complained a great deal about the thorn in the flesh which made things so difficult for him. He urgently prayed God to remove this thorn. We can no longer even guess what kind of a thorn it was. Paul was short in stature and unimpressive to look at: he complained about this in one of his letters. He could well have said that he was not very suitable to be an apostle. 'God, for heaven's sake choose a large and impressive person to proclaim this message to the world. I am incapable of doing what you want of me...' And then there was his thorn in the flesh which tormented him so. Was it a chronic illness? A psychological weakness? A temptation of some kind? Whatever it may have been, it seems that God thought this goad necesary, since Paul still got the same answer: 'My grace must be enough for you, my power is made perfect in weakness' (II Cor.12.9).

Presumably he would not have become 'Saint' Paul without the goad of his suffering which the Lord gave him like spurs for the race. We should feel our weaknesses and know our limitations before God – that makes us keen of hearing, sensitive, humble. We must be poor before God, but know that all is grace. Ill health can sometimes be the condition for a spiritual revival and flourishing, for full awareness. We have plenty of instances of this. There are infinitely many things which robustly healthy people cannot grasp, which they find so difficult. But think of the power there is in the mystery of suffering! From antiquity down to our day these great sufferers have lived among us. Pascal, one of the most profound and versatile thinkers in human history, was infirm and soon fell sick, but he left us his *Pensées*, which are among the finest pearls that human genius has ever produced. These pearls of wisdom occurred to him between migraines and fearful liver disease, and he died at the age of thirty-nine. So defect or loss on one level becomes gain on another, higher level. All is grace. The state of our health never determines our spiritual productivity.

We might think of the invalid Blondel, or Bergson, the Jewish Nobel prizewinner. Or the blind Lazarist Pouget, to whom the young intellectuals of France went for counsel. Or the Egyptian Muslim Taha Hussein, one of the most significant scholars and writers in the Arab world. He would probably never have become the great Taha Hussein had he not been blinded at the age of seven. His work of staggering sensitivity, refinement and depth is rooted in this life of suffering. His eyes were closed to our sunlight, but were opened to another light and saw things which we are not able to experience. He wrote forty books, and his finest, *Al-Aijam*, has meanwhile appeared in Russian and Danish, Indonesian and Chinese, among other languages. He died in 1973.

Let us remain in Egypt, but look back to the time of the Pharaohs, to the year 1350 BC. Not many people know much about Akenaton, the social pharaoh, religious genius and founder of monotheism. Moses was influenced by him, and many psalms in our Bible go back to his inspiration. This great man was a physical wreck; he lived, thought, wrote poetry and worked with his health completely ruined: he died at the age of thirty.

Geniuses in particular and spiritual figures generally do not need health or special privileges. We should never let a weak condition be an excuse for sitting back, but rouse ourselves and offer our intention to God. Then he will help us to begin it, and bring it to an end.

Think of the simple spirit of the Curé d'Ars, later St Jean-Marie Vianney. Despite his ardent desire to become a priest he was virtually incapable of grasping arguments, though he was borne up by a rocklike faith. Although the academically-minded advised him to abandon his dream, he made the attempt. Then by grace he passed the examination, was ordained priest, was allowed to give absolution. And the Curé d'Ars became the best-known and most beloved spiritual advisor of his century, if not of all centuries. People flocked by the thousand from all over Europe to his simple sermons – especially the intellectual world, including learned men and philosophers. Could not this man have said to himself, 'Priest? A splendid idea! Unfortunately I don't have the equipment'? But he said something else, perhaps, 'The little that I contribute will bear fruit if grace touches it – and that is what I shall ask for.' He offered his five loaves of bread and two fishes to the Lord, and asked him to bless these gifts. And God's blessing fell on this paltry gift a thousandfold and a hundred thousandfold – beyond all expectations. Here is the wonder of grace: great things can perhaps perfect themselves in weakness, as Paul writes – through the simplest instruments by means of poverty.

Is understanding other people also a gift? In understanding one 'gives' something. And it is very often those who have had to drink the bitter gall of suffering who now understand their fellow human beings. If you want to sense someone else's suffering and understand the particularly deep realities of existence, then you must be made porous to it by undergoing suffering. If God wants to shake people awake to teach them a particular lesson, then he often begins by blessing them with what in Arabic is called a *mussiba*, a piece of misfortune. So the Jesuit order begins with the broken leg of a man called Ignatius Loyola. Had he not had this painful leg with its unpleasant consequences at a particular point in his life, then today there would not be a single Jesuit in the world, instead of the 26,000 that there are.

In the end, all is gain. Look through your personal life to see whether you can find any roses blossoming among the refuse. If we lose something at one level, we gain it at another. At one point I prayed to the Lord to shake a particular person by a *mussiba*, to scare him out of his permanent coma. He had sunk into himself and was blocked off by his egotism, too dull and incapable of feeling and understanding the most basic need in his surroundings, and was acting accordingly.

What can we really know about the nature of a misfortune, about its essence, its meaning, its message and its consequences? And what do we really know of happiness? What is ultimately good for us or bad for us? Only God knows. There is an Arabic proverb which goes, 'Do not fear evil, for it may bring you good.'

In the context of this Arabic wisdom, here is a legend, a parable from China.

A wise farmer had a son, a horse and a neighbour. One morning the son rode off to market in the city, but in the hills the horse threw him and wandered off. So the son came back by himself. 'What a misfortune,' said the neighbour. 'How do you know?', said the farmer.

The next day, the son set off to look for the lost horse. He found it, and in addition brought back a splendid wild stallion – proud at his skill in catching him. 'What good fortune,' said the neighbour. 'How do you know?', said the farmer.

The next morning, the son began to break in the stallion, but it threw him, and the son broke an arm. 'What a misfortune,' said the neighbour. 'How do you know?', said the farmer.

The next morning the king's recruiting officer came to the village to conscript the young men for war. Because of his temporary incapacity the son escaped military service. 'What good fortune,' said the neighbour. 'How do you know?', said the farmer.

The next morning... The next morning...

Fortune or misfortune, how do we know? We need to accept in faith what God has planned for us. The saying 'all is grace' comes from St Paul, and St Augustine added, 'even sin'. In fact sin, evil *par excellence*, can become the source of good, indeed the greatest good; and we believe that and understand it when we look on the cross.

Do we not find the story of many former sinners even among the saints? Only grace can bring about such a transformation. St Augustine, whom I have just quoted, did not write this sentence while theorizing and theologizing between his tractates, starting from a purely intellectual concept, but from the abundance of his own practical experience of life and suffering. In his famous *Confessions* he records more than thirty years of his life which in his estimation he spent as a sinner. The founder of our Jesuit order, too, was bent on pleasure until his conversion, as was Francis Xavier, who was later to become the great missionary to the Far East. And there was Charles de Foucauld's loose life-style in Paris, with all his diversions. And all the rest... Perhaps many of them could not rise to the state of holiness unless they had experimented in their lives with sin and subsequently had tasted the misery of the sinner. It seems to me that sin tears something open in the human heart; it opens up a division through which grace finds entry. Then those involved experience a radical spiritual transformation, a conversion. Whether they would ever have been capable of discovering the same depths of God, the same nearness of God, of discovering love, without the background of their experience of sin suffered in body and soul, is something that none of us can know – nor did they themselves. If we are really convinced that sin – and nothing worse can happen to us – can be a way that ends in God, then we no longer need to be anxious, since all is grace, all is gain.

But we are so often Pharisees! We fancy that we are free from sin... and then an armour of self-satisfaction encloses us and cuts us off from the light of grace. We think that we do not need anything. The crust on the essence of our being shuts us off from our environment and is so impenetrable that not even grace can shine through it. Withdrawn into our self-satisfaction, we do not even long for redemption, for otherwise we would open ourselves to it. How can grace reach us? It will not break our free will. So presumably it is sin which creates this salutary wound. The Lord allows it as a divide through which he can find access to our hearts. Formerly we were too smooth and too orderly – so much so that we pleased ourselves.

But if we are going to offer ourselves to God, we need to do so soon. We must not wait for the day when we are spotless and worthy of this encounter, since there are the morally bent among us who have no self-confidence (or not enough) and a distorted relationship to God, the Father. No, we must not wait. Some people tell me that they won't start praying until they have got rid of their faults and weaknesses. And then I prophesy to them that they will spend their lives waiting. But above all, God is wholly other. He is not someone whom one visits in a dinner jacket. So we must go as we are, now, straight away. And if we fall, we must get up and keep going towards him. We must be like the prodigal son who heads home and considers what he will say to his father: 'Father, I have sinned against heaven and before you, and am no more worthy to be called your son.'

But it is not like this. The Lord will receive us as his children, always and in every situation, precisely as we are at this moment. The love of God which we experience knows no deeper relationship and no higher quality than the concept of our childlikeness. We are children of God. We stand before him with empty hands and sometimes like the prodigal son, stained and broken, exhausted and guilt-ridden. But beyond the shadows, within we remain profoundly God's children. We have no higher quality than this: it is the supreme quality that we can possess as human beings, and grace gives it to us. The love of the Father is pure grace.

We need always to compare this inner relationship with the father of a family who is cuddling a child which has a bad conscience. The fact of the father-child relationship is enough to show that the child is accepted, is loved; that it is understood at critical times and, if necessary, is given its father's forgiveness. A loving father does not just close one eye, but both – we have all experienced that.

The prodigal son had squandered his father's money and property and abused his trust. But now the father was not interested in any discussions about the cirucmstances and reasons for this breach of trust, but in unbounded joy ran to meet his son when he saw him coming, and embraced him.

There is no doubt that the father loved his son greatly, for the son had caused him infinite pain, anxiety and suffering. That is always the case. If you are a teacher or have children of your own, there will always be the *enfant terrible* who is closest to your heart. While grieving you he will raise your spirits. By contrast, the other son in the Gospel, the loyal and diligent one, had claims

146]

on his father: he thought that his loyalty and obedience gave him rights. This son will never have understood what was happening here, what the prodigal son was now experiencing. He himself was too clean, too self-satisfied and too loyal to understand the absolute and free offering of a father's love which the prodigal son was now enjoying. He could not have this experience of grace.

We need to reflect quietly on this parable, since in my view it is the most profound of any in the Gospels. It is our story. Nevertheless, all too many of us believe that we have to prepare carefully for our encounter with God, that we have to smarten ourselves up and above all purify ourselves in penitence before taking part in the mass and communicating. People think that only then will the Father embrace them: only if they are pure. But what a mistake that is!

Suppose that on his journey home the son had been told in a distant welcome from his father that first he had to clean himself up and put on respectable clothes before he came to give a detailed explanation of himself! It is just not true that we may not appear before God unclean; that is not said anywhere. Moreover, not only may we come as we are and God will receive us immediately, but God will take us to his heart spontaneously and embrace us, as in the parable, and we shall be clean, through him. For it is not human beings who cleanse themselves before going to God, but God who cleanses human beings if they come to him.

The love of God is absolute love. We are not given it by making ourselves fit for it, but it is directed towards us, shines through us and purifies us; it not only purifies, but ennobles and changes. So I would stress once again that we need to avoid those who want to drum into us that we must go to confession before communion, which I know is still the strict demand of a number of churches and certain priests. We all have particular weaknesses and particular faults. I too go to confession now and then, but I allow myself the freedom to choose how often. In earlier times compulsory confession tormented all of us, but that is past. No, I go to confession with the aim of being transformed, for the love of God precedes everything.

'Lord, I am not worthy', we say before every communion. No, I was never worthy to receive the host, God himself, on any day of my life. If I wanted to wait until I was worthy of this pure and infinite love of God I would have to wait to the end of my life and beyond – to the end of time.

So in the Coptic mass the faithful say before communion, 'Given to us for the forgiveness of sins'. The body of Christ is *given* to us, for all is grace. The Catholic priest chooses between the words, 'Whoever eats of this bread will live for ever', and, 'Blessed are those who are invited to the marriage feast of the lamb'. Those who receive communion are blessed, blessed in the working of divine grace. The word was revealed to John as the 'true word of God' (Rev.19.9). Contact with Christ in the host has a purifying, transforming, ennobling and redemptive effect. We do not go to him because we are pure, but because we want to *become* pure and worthy of him. He is the one who saves. The name Jesus is derived from the Hebrew *Yeshua* and means YHWH helps, God saves. Jesus is called the Saviour because he *is* the Saviour; it lies in his nature, his being, his person, his personality that he is the one who saves us. We do not go to a vague cosmic creator spirit, but we go to the Lord of the world who has revealed himself and who loves men and women, revealed and manifested in Jesus Christ. He showed himself to us as gentleness and meekness, as mercy and loving forgiveness. He is the God who saves men and women.

That is the revelation of the working of grace; that is redemption and sanctification. However, unfortunately we are all still too caught up in the philosophical, intellectual Old Testament, and in addition pharisaically think that we are more or less free of sin and in accord with God. But in truth, as human beings we shall never be in accord with God, but will remain debtors who are unable to repay him.

Still, all is grace. Let us remember the parable of the servant who is deeply in debt (Matt.18). He was in the red to his king to the tune of ten thousand talents, and he would never ever have been able to repay this debt. So in desperation he threw himself at his master's feet, and asked for forgiveness – and his master forgave him the debt! That is the gospel! And if we do not understand it in any other way, at least let us understand it in terms of these parables, which are strong and crystal-clear, for the Lord composed them for us to grasp and understand the message of salvation. Word for word we find in them what grace is. If we have the courage to encounter God not only with empty hands but with hands stained with guilt, with a long past, laden with the weight of faults of every kind, with mediocrity and weakness of character, then we are on the right way. Believe!

Here I think above all of Martin Luther. He was a man with very deep intuitions. To a certain extent he was right to oppose the Catholics by stressing so much the completely free gift of justification, that concept in Christian theology which relates to the restoration of the unity of human beings with their creator, which has been destroyed by sin. Since then, Protestant theology has called this pardon a pure gift of God which is given to human beings only in faith. Christians are justified solely by the grace of God, without any merit of their own. Luther, too, says that all is grace. Protestants believe that human beings cannot of themselves re-establish contact with God, but only on the basis of the divine forgiveness which they receive as grace in faith, 'by faith alone, by grace alone, *sola fide, sola gratia*'.

We also find the same thing in Paul. In several splendid chapters of his letter to the Romans he urgently writes about the value of grace; there we find his marvellous doctrine of justification. Paul proclaims the grace of God, that we are justified without our own doing through his grace, thanks to our redemption in Jesus Christ. He also writes to the Galatians to the same effect. Human beings are justified by faith and through grace, and not on the basis of their works. So-called good works then flow from grace as the fruit, the consequence of justification, as the outworking of divine forgiveness and purification; they are not its condition. This theological view, which was also that of Luther, is very deep and very important. Luther gave a great deal to the Catholic church, and especially since the Second Vatican Council we are in a position to appreciate the full depth of his teaching.

And while we are talking of Protestants, here I am reminded of another important theologian and philosopher, Paul Tillich. He was born in Germany and emigrated to America in 1933. This is what he had to say about grace.

We cannot transform our lives, unless we allow them to be transformed by the stroke of grace. Grace strikes us when we walk through the dark valley of a meaningless and empty life. It strikes us when we feel that our separation is deeper than usual, because we have violated another life, a life which we loved, or from which we were estranged. It strikes us when our disgust for our own being, our indifference, our weakness, our hostility, and our lack of direction and composure have become intolerable to us. It strikes us when, year after year, the longed-for perfection of life does not appear, when the old compulsions reign within us as they have for decades, when despair destroys all joy and courage.

Sometimes at that moment a wave of light breaks into our darkness, and it is as though a voice were saying, 'You are accepted!' If that happens to us, we experience grace.

After such an experience we may not be better than before, and we may not believe more than before. But everything is transformed, changed. In that moment grace conquers sin, and reconciliation bridges the gulf of estrangement. And nothing is demanded of this experience, no religious or moral or intellectual presupposition, nothing but acceptance.

This splendid text is illuminating for me in its greatness and beauty, and it expresses to me the innermost depths of Christian teaching. I am accepted as I am, in my poverty and emptiness, in my distress and anguish and with all my mistakes. 'Yes, you are accepted.' I believe that what has been put so simply here relates to the most important experience of grace which we can have in our existence, and this message may serve men and women as a source of liberation. We are all brothers and sisters of Christ, we are all children of God, and therefore we are accepted. The revelation of grace is a shattering one.

But we should note one thing. Justification by God means not only that God receives in grace sinners or weaklings and turns to them in love but essentially leaves them sinners and weaklings. It means infinitely more. It means transformation. And here unfortunately we find the difference between the Catholic and the Orthodox Christian conception on the one hand and the Protestant conception on the other. Our brothers and sisters who are Protestants believe that human beings are illuminated by grace or veiled in it; a cloak comes over sinners to cover their sin. But that means that their sin continues under the cloak and that despite the divine working of grace and being accepted by the Father, men and women nevertheless remain sinners. The confidence of Catholic and Orthodox Christians in the efficacy of grace extends still further; they do not believe that their guilt is merely covered and their soul illuminated by the light of God, but they firmly believe that they are newly created by the grace of Christ:

My legal status is restored;
The initial state of holiness is restored;

I am raised up as a new being.

This miracle which makes people righteous takes place in a constant dynamic process of the working of grace. Catholic and Orthodox Christians believe that sins are really taken away; for them that is the embodiment of redemption, the comprehensive meaning of the message of salvation. Grace transforms, recreates, renews, brings completely new children of God into being. Damaged, weakened, marked, we were taken into the furnace of the heart of Jesus and left it as gleaming gold bars. We are truly redeemed.

Redemption is a new creation, a radical change of being, a transformation at the heart of our being. God creates us with his own hands for the second time, for grace transforms men and women to the roots of their being. It not only covers all evil, lovingly enwraps the former person we were, but it says, 'Behold, I make all things new' (Revelation 21.5).

And that is the new and in fact redemptive element in this message to the world, which is why we call it the 'good' news that we are to proclaim to all men and women. And we should not do so timidly and irresolutely or in passing, but passionately and very directly. In the cross on Golgotha the whole universe was poured into the furnace and remoulded. That is why the Gospel of Matthew reports that on Good Friday darkness came over the whole land for three hours, the earth quaked and the rocks split. Elsewhere we read of such signs only in the Apocalypse: they are signs of the downfall of the old world. Here something breaks, something dies. On the death of Jesus the whole universe collapsed inwardly and died with him. It is the hour of the death of the old creation, and the hour of the birth of the new creation, which one day will shine in splendour before us all: at the end of history, when a new heaven spreads over a new earth. This is what John experienced in a holy vision which transcended time and which he recorded for us in his Revelation or Apocalypse, in accordance with the words which he heard: 'Write, for these words are true and faithful'.

We can also read in the Second Letter of Peter, 'The heavens will be kindled and dissolved, and the elements will melt with fire. But according to his promise we wait for new heavens and a new earth in which righteousness dwells' (3.12b-13).

Righteousness – for all is grace, all is gain. To end this book I want to express the wish that this new life, promising light and harmony, may finally conquer the lack of peace in our hearts and spirits and give birth to a peace which surpasses all other forms of peace, all anxiety, all toil and torment, all questions and counter-questions, every kind of wisdom, every proof and counter-proof, every reflection, every doubt.

What I mean is a spiritual peace, a clear inner heaven. This is what Christ meant when he said in his blessing, 'Peace be with you'. And if we keep alive deep in our hearts the conviction that all is grace and all is gain, then there will no longer be any reason for fears of any kind, for the transforming power of the death of Christ will bring about this miracle of peace.

Peace I leave with you; my peace I give to you. Let not your hearts be troubled, neither let them be afraid (John 14.27).

The peace which the world gives is based on human logic and the human capacity for judgment, on human motivations, values and possibilities. That is why it so quickly vanishes and leaves our spirits abandoned. But the peace of Christ is of quite another order; it lies beyond all human evidence and certainty. This peace exists beyond all possibilities, but also beyond our lack of capacity, since it is borne up on the wings of blind faith and the deep certainty that God is and always will be, that he is wiser than the wisest man and stronger than the deepest sin, and overcomes evil in his love. 'Be of good cheer, I have overcome the world' (John 16.33).

This peace which is to fill us is not based on what we do or do not do, nor is it based on what we are, but only on God, on God's grace and his love. So there can be no power in the world which could threaten or destroy this spiritual peace.

At the depths of the Christian revelation we find the message that human history is a history of redemption, a history of grace, in which everything is redeemed, transformed and shaped anew, for 'where sin increased, grace abounded all the more', as Paul preached to the Romans. Since then we may assume that all is grace – in the last resort, even sin.

We might ask ourselves whether things could not have been different. Could the love of God have flowed over us to this amazing extent even if we had not been abounding in sin? There seems to be a kind of time-conditioned historical necessity for the existence of sin. Perhaps that is what Christ meant when he said,

'There must be offences.' Is that perhaps the ultimate significance of what we call original sin?

For we must never forget that sin, too, and perhaps sin in particular, manifests God to men and women. We cannot experience and understand what sin really is unless we see it in the light of God. Only through redemption can we learn to understand it in retrospect. God's redemption of humankind is at the same time an uncovering and disclosure of human sin and its obliteration – through Jesus Christ. Human beings could not bear the burden of their guilt were it not revealed to them in the mystery of Christ. It is useless for men and women to know their guilt unless at the same time and to the same degree they consciously experience the grace and love of Christ which saves them.

Last of all, a meditation to remind us of the truth of grace:

Lord, give me to the full the knowledge of the work of your grace in this world. Then your grace will also begin to work in me as a source of peace.

Help me to understand that despite my faults and weaknesses, my defects and limitations, you have invited me to the greatest adventure of all – adventure with you.

I still hesitate to accept your offer; I do not dare to take your hand. But I feel your impulses which move my heart, and I hear your gentle call in me to be bold. Indeed you encourage me in these days to find a new beginning in my life and to want to commit myself for this world.

You know that I am poor in resources and bring little with me. I am nothing special. But with the little I have I shall be able to do all things, for you will bring them to completion.

So I give you my five loaves and my two fishes, and I give you my weaknesses and the little that I have. Take it, Lord, and transform it into food for many, perhaps for thousands.

Then let this cheerful faith dominate all my actions and thoughts, beyond the errors and mistakes which I shall certainly make. Set me up when I fall, strengthen me when I fail, and make me confident of finding a new beginning.

Above all strengthen my faith in your grace more and more. Let me draw strength from this source which sprang from the hill of Golgotha, and which flowed into the boundless ocean of grace.

Let the deep certainty of acceptance sink into my heart. Above my being and action let me at all times sense your love and find your peace, your divine peace which is beyond time, which transcends all other forms of peace.

You have left us peace. Help us to understand it. Let it fill my soul and guide me to the knowledge of the last word of the revelation of grace: 'The love of God is at work behind all appearances.'